The Story of Early Estes Park

By Enos A. Mills

With Contributions by
Flora J. R. T. Stanley
and
Esther Burnell Mills

Temporal Mechanical Press
Longs Peak, Colorado

"A Tenderfoot's First Summer in the Rockies" by Flora J. R. T.
Stanley Copyright © 1999 Stanley Museum, Kingfield, Maine.
For more information, contact: The Stanley Museum, P.O. Box 77,
Kingfield, Maine, 04947. 207-265-2729
www.stanleymuseum.org

Photographs by the author.
Temporal Mechanical Press
a division of Enos Mills Cabin
6760 Highway 7
Estes Park, CO 80517-6404
www.enosmills.com
enosmillscbn@earthlink.net

ISBN 978-1-928878-05-6

TABLE OF CONTENTS

FOREWORDS

This booklet is not the work of a scholar, but of a guide. It is written because a guide book is needed, and for the purpose of conveniently recording The Story of Estes Park.

I am under obligations to Harper & Brothers for the privilege of quoting from "A Ragged Register", by Miss Anna E. Dickinson, and to G. P. Putnam's Sons for allowing me to make extracts from "A Lady's Life in the Rocky Mountains", by Isabella L. Bird-Bishop.

I am indebted to many pioneers and early visitors for letters and interviews, and to Honorable Platt Rogers, William S. Cooper and Abner E. Sprague for special contributions, and to H. C. Rogers and J. A. McGuire for important suggestions.

But above all these, there is one to whom I am more indebted, and to him,

ROBERT W. JOHNSON.

this little booklet is inscribed.

ENOS A. MILLS

Longs Peak Inn, Estes Park, Colorado,
February 3, 1905

Den. Colo, Jan. 21 1905

Dear Mills,
I'm scarcely ever in
Denver now, & have only just rec'd
your letter yesterday.
My P. O. is Box 2, Sedalia. &
we go for mail about once a week.
Am very busy and am so tired after
I get through at night. I have given up
writing letters to everyone, and everything
else in fact. I took on a string of 45 head,
mostly for polo, have two riders, and
we three ride them out daily, expect
to have everything sold by July 1st. Its not
horse raising, not by a damn sight, just
an experience.
Glad to hear of your growing literary
success, stick to it. I may be there myself
in earnest, after this stuff. and be denced glad
to show up at the Long's Peak House, foot free.
Think your letter heads ripping; and
envelopes rotten, Long's Peak should stand out in
simple & eloquent
lines. Now its unintelligible and sloppy (excuse critique)
In reply to your book venture, would
say; I shall be glad to put up $150 or
perhaps, 200 whenever you need it. If I could in anything meantime.
Have no suggestions, except for myself
would rather have scenery pictures, than
too many of the Estes family, who as I
understand it, are entirely uninteresting,
to the avove except for supplying a name to
the most beautiful mountain valley I've
seen in Colo, With all kinds of goode
wishes
Ever, yours sincerely,
Robert H. Hudson

-ii-
Come & see me if you get down here.

My P. O. is Box 2, Sedalia. & we go for mail about once a week.

Am very busy and am so tired after I get through at night, I have given up writing letters to everyone, and everything else in fact. I took on a string of 45 head, mostly for polo, have two riders, and we three ride them out daily, expect to have everything sold by July 1st. It's not horse raising, not by a damn sight, just an experience.

Glad to hear of your growing literary success, stick to it. I may be there myself in earnest, after this horse stuff, and be deuced glad to show up at the Long's Peak House, frost free.

Think your letter heads ripping; and envelopes rotten. Long's Peak should stand out in simple & eloquent lines. Now it's unintelligible and sloppy (excuse critique)

In reply to your book venture. would say. I shall be glad to put up $150 or perhaps 200 whenever you need it. If I'm early in anything meantime.

Have no suggestions, except for myself would rather have scenery pictures, than too many of the Ester family. who as I understand it, are entirely uninteresting to the author except for supplying a name to the most beautiful mountain valley I've seen in Colo, With all kinds of goode wishes

Ever, yours sincerely,
Robert W. Judson

Come & see me if you get down here.

FOREWORD
Reviewing the Past

Picture Estes Park two hundred years ago—without a single habitation, without even a name! By foot, horseback, wagon, stage and automobile, through the years, trappers, hunters, settlers, explorers and tourists found their way. The merest trail became a barely passable road, and this, with increasing use, became wider and wider, and finally our highways.

It seems a fitting time to recall the early days and make the spirit of the pioneers come alive. We are fortunate to have the story by Enos Mills, for not only was he an early settler, but he knew many of the old-timers who preceded him and had their experiences first hand. He had the gift of linking the past with the present, and the insight to envision great promise for the future.

Interwoven in the development of Estes Park is the life story of Enos Mills. The stimulus of the country is great—his mind expanded in reaching out to comprehend the whole of what he saw. Without realizing it, he created new concepts for the future enjoyment of this mountain wonderland by others, and set about to train himself for the part he was eventually to play in the drama.

Long's Peak drew Mills like a magnet. It was both a challenge and a friend; he knew it in all moods, by day and by night, and in all seasons of the year. It was not enough, however, just to take people to the summit—he wanted to share with them his enthusiasms for the wealth of interests along the way. When he mentioned that they were climbing through Life Zones comparable to journeying to the Arctic Circle, it gave special meaning to the birds, trees, flowers and animals seen. In addition it was often the added interest which held parties together, and enabled all to successfully reach their goal.

So great was Mills' zeal to have the whole region of

Estes Park better known, he became Park correspondent for the Denver papers, and through the 1890's contributed articles on the scenery, forest and wild life, illustrated with photographs. Nor did he neglect the human-nature element. He rode many miles horseback collecting "society" news at the various hotels, for the comings and goings of prominent people is prone to be an incentive to visit new scenes.

Mills soon found himself being called upon to lecture over the state. His subject was usually "Our Friends, the Trees", stressing their economic value to the nation—conserving rainfall, preventing soil erosion and moderating the climate. Forest-fires had devastated large areas in the west and he hoped to prevent this waste by instilling in others his own intense love for trees. His talks were a combination of common-sense and sentiment. He knew his subject and presented it with all the deepest feeling of his nature.

Mills was an easy speaker and never failed to hold his audience, whether it was an auditorium full of restless children, a progressive Chamber of Commerce, a Woman's Club, or a gathering in Washington—where President Taft could not be persuaded to leave for an engagement until he had heard the end of Mills' bear stories.

These lecture tours took Mills from coast to coast. In June, 1906, while making an address in St. Paul, he received a telegram saying the main building of Longs Peak Inn had burned to the ground. Many invaluable bird and animal negatives, and hotel supplies he had purchased for the season, were a part of the loss. But on the way home he formulated plans for rebuilding. He was ready for tourists July 4th.

There were acres of standing fire-killed trees on the surrounding mountains, in an excellent state of preservation, many beautifully carved and colored or showing unusual twisted grain. Getting this material hauled down, and persuading carpenters to follow his plans presented problems, but the result was something new and artistic in rustic architecture, and fitted into the scenes.

His twenty years of adventures with snowslides, racing avalanches, trailing grizzly bear and watching beaver, gave Mills the desire to write, and the enthusiasm with which these magazine articles were read made an incentive for the books that followed. He wanted more people to know Colorado, and any new project that would encourage their coming had his active support. Many of the business people who followed him into the area speak of his generosity in helping them get a start.

Already the idea of a National Park along the higher slopes of the Continental Divide, from the Colorado-Wyoming border to Pike's Peak, was formulating in his mind. But this area, much of it above timberline, and of no value for grazing or lumber, was controlled by the National Forest Service, which made strenuous opposition to relinquishing any of it, even for better uses. The territory originally proposed was reduced so as to include only a twenty-five mile expanse of rugged peaks west of Estes Park. After six years of persistence, writing, lecturing and campaigning, the Bill creating the Rocky Mountain National Park was passed by Congress, January, 1915.

An editorial in The Denver Post expressed the general sentiment:

"It was Enos A. Mills, who conceived the idea of conserving nature's wonderful workmanship in the Long's Peak region by placing it in the keeping of the United States Government, and, single-handed, he set out to accomplish this result. Single-handed, he brought it about, for all the forces that have contributed to the victory were lined up through his efforts. Others have helped, to be sure, but it was by Enos Mills' persistent labor that they were made supporters of the movement. So let Colorado take off its hat to Enos Mills, who has nationalized Colorado's scenery, in which every citizen is a stockholder and dividend participant."

To encourage city-dwellers to go into the wilderness,

Mills had added cabins to Longs Peak Inn with steam heat and private bath, and had a six-months season. In 1916 further additions doubled the lobby and dining-room capacity. The Nature Museum, with his collection of unusual specimens of beaver work and twisted trees, flower and tree exhibits, brought people from near and far. Mills was available to answer questions or direct climbing parties, but took time to introduce new guests to the ways of the beaver, or to find the first Columbine, blue fringed gentian or red wood lily. This informal nature study, which he sometimes called his "Trail School," was the forerunner of the Ranger-Naturalist service in the National Parks.

In 1918 Enos Mills improved his own cabin on the Inn grounds—to accommodate his bride! I had been a guest at the Inn, part-time secretary, homesteader and nature guide[1]. Our cabin had further additions in 1919 on the arrival of our baby daughter. Enda was the greatest possible joy to her father, and her response to his companionship seemed to bring out the tenderest side of his nature. Even the stories he was writing seemed to emphasize the home life and habits of animals, and the bringing-up of their young.

But not all was well with the Park in Mills' estimation. Stipulations in the Bill creating the Park had been violated: "No lands located within the park boundaries now held in private, municipal or State ownership shall be affected by or subject to the provisions of this act." The controversial transportation monopoly granted by the National Park Service was over state-built roads, and even in some instances over roads built by the pioneers. It became a matter for litigation—litigation that continued for twelve years—until finally, under political pressure,

---

[1]

Editor's note: Esther was the first woman licensed as a nature guide by the National Park Service.

the State ceded its roads to the United States Government.

Working patiently, Mills never gave up hope of winning in his fight for competitive transportation. The region had grown up and flourished under the initiative of the local people, and there was adequate service both to and through the Park. Mills had seen the results of monopolistic concessions in other National Parks and felt they would be detrimental to the continued development of the Rocky Mountain National Park, and for the freedom of people using it.

It was a gallant fight for the region he loved, and the many who had seen the justice of his cause mourned the more deeply at his death. For Enos Mills passed away September 21, 1922, at Longs Peak, Colorado.

An editorial in the Rocky Mountain News caught the spirit of the man and his life work:

"If Enos Mills had lived in a city he would have spent himself trying to reform it and fighting the people's battles. Fortunate for him and the West, which he loved passionately and understandingly, he had within him the soul of the Pioneer. He gave his thought and his reforming instinct, which was very strong in him, toward the preservation of Nature. To him it was a religion and he pursued it as such. He wrote of what he observed in his long tramps through the mountains in summer and winter. He had the faculty of making others see it almost as he saw it. His fame had spread widely—first of all he engaged himself in having Congress create the Rocky Mountain National Park. He knew all the ground and what it contained. After the park was created he did not like the way bureaucracy was doing with it from Washington and he took up the cudgels for the freedom of all national parks. Whether he was right or wrong he believed in his cause and was without ulterior motives—Estes Park and the name of Enos Mills were inseparably linked. Something distinctive has been taken out of the heart of the Rocky Mountains. He has joined a band of noble brothers on the other side of the range."

Enos Mills' unselfish devotion to Estes Park was for the whole of it—not for any one peak, lake or mountain pass more than another. The inspiration he had received from these stirring scenes and experiences he gave back a hundredfold, in his books and in his wide personal contacts. His great legacy he shared with the world and his influence will continue to be felt down through the years.

ESTHER BURNELL MILLS

Mrs. Enos A. Mills
June, 1959

DONALD MACGREGOR
ESTES PARK, COLORADO

Estes Park, Colorado,
June 6, 1957.

Dear Mrs. Mills,

Thank you for the photograph. Have pictures of the same type so know it was taken long years ago. Do not know the man in the picture.

Am curious for another reason. Could this be my grandfather? He was dead many years before I was born. At the time Mr. Mills was writing the little book about the history of Estes Park, he called on my father at the family home in Denver and asked him to loan him family records for use in the book.

What records my father did loan him were destroyed presumably in the first fire that destroyed Longs Peak Inn. No evidence any were used in preparing the book as my father grandfather's name was Alexander Quiner MacGregor. Mr. Mills calls him R. Q. MacGregor and seems to have established that name for him. Have no idea how the error arose.

The photograph could have been loaned with the last records and now have come back to me. Stranger things have happened. Do not suppose you have any further information about it.

A strange spring here. Nearly went under taking care of my cows and horses thru the heavy snows from April 2nd thru the fifteenth. In early May was drowned out heavy rains. My meadow is wet normally, the cows know the safe places to graze. After the rains was dragging them out of the bogs all over the meadow. Grass is the latest I have ever known it on the hillsides. Maybe the droughth did kill it.

Best regards.

Yours,

Muriel MacGregor

INTRODUCTION

This volume is the consequence of dissecting all previous editions and selecting the essence of the very early times spent in Estes Park. Enos A. Mills' first book, *The Story of Estes Park and a Guide Book* is, as always, a glorious experience to explore the Estes Park of the past.

Enos did not include the *Guide* section in his second edition *The Story of Estes Park.* Nor did the subsequent editions *The Story of Estes Park and Grand Lake, The Rocky Mountain National Park Memorial Edition, Early Estes Park,* and *The Story of Early Estes Park Rocky Mountain National Park and Grand Lake.*

We have tried to remain faithful to the original "paleface" names of areas, rock formations and canyons of this time period, simply because we can not keep up with the recent explosion of confusing name changes.

We have added a few new goodies we hope you will enjoy.

We thank the Stanley Museum of Estes Park, Colorado and Kingfield, Maine for graciously allowing us to include a portion of Flora J.R.T. Stanley's personal perspective of Estes Park.

This volume is dedicated to the future generations who will inherit The Circle.

THE STORY OF
EARLY ESTES PARK

The first glimpse of the park never fails to arouse the dullest traveler; and those who frequently behold it from the entrance find the scene as welcome as an old song.

Estes Park has a length of twelve miles and a varied width from one to three miles. Its outline is beautifully irregular—being broken by invading ridges, between which the park swells out into glades, basins and glens.

It is an artistic realm. From the entrance one looks down on an irregular depression surrounded by high, forest-walled mountains—this depression an undulating green meadow with great pines sprinkled over it. Some spaces are without a tree and others covered with a grove. A few rocky points and cliffs picturesquely arise in the midst; lines of aspen and willow trim the brooks; and the Big Thompson River, sweeping in great folds from side to side, goes majestically across it.

The continental divide forms the western boundary, and for several miles the great, jagged snowy range stands splendidly above it. Great ridges covered with a dark green plush of pines, comes down into the park from the range. One of these ridges, Cathedral, is royally crowned with nature's statuary–domes, cliffs, spires and far-reaching granite columns.

At the southwest corner of the park—the Glacier Gorge country—is a section destined to become as famous as the Yosemite. Now it is an almost untrodden wild. This region consists of several canyons lying between the vertebra of the high, broken and snowy continental divide. Lock Vale is the most noted one. The lower portion of this canyon is ice-sculpted—and the upper portion, deep and rough, contains alpinic lakes, silken meadows, snow banks, ice fields, colored cliffs, tree clumps and wild cataracts that "leap in glory."

The park has the beautiful and the sublime. In it bees hum and beavers build; the wood thrush, unseen, gives a silvery melody to the forest depth, and butterflies with painted wings circle the sunny air. Mountain Sheep with classic pose watch from the cliffs, eagles soar the blue, speckled beauties sprinkle the clear streams and the varied voice of the coyote echoes when the afterglow falls.

Beautiful wild flowers flourish and are mostly of bright color. Each season nearly a thousand varieties perfume the air and open their "bannered bosoms to the sun". They crown the streams, wave on the hills, shine in woodland vistas and color the snow edge. Daisies, orchids, tiger lilies, blue fringed gentians, wild red roses, mariposas, adorn every space and nook.

Up between the domes on top of Cathedral Ridge is Gem Lake. It is only a little crystal pool set in ruddy granite with a few evergreens on its rocky shore. It is one of the rare gems of lake world.

Albert Bierstadt used to paint and dream on the shores of a lake which now bears his name. Bierstadt Lake has twenty acres of clear, elliptical surface in the midst of great woods. Between golden pond lilies its enameled surface splendidly reflects clouds and sky, peak and snow field.

Chasm Lake is in a deep canyon with 3,000 feet of Long's Peak granite standing over it. The lake is a quarter of a mile in length and is deep, clear and cold. It is 11,000 feet above sea level. Its shores are piled with ice, snow and great fragments that gravity has torn from above. About the lake conies, ptarmigan—Arctic Quail—live, and many beautiful varieties of sub-Arctic flora grow. On the whole, the scene is awesome and sublime. There are not many places where one can gaze up a natural 3,000 foot wall.

Many glaciers have left their mark on the Park mountains. Some canyons are polished or eroded. There is much glacial debris, scores of lateral, medial and terminal moraines. There are moraines 500 feet high and a mile in length composed entirely of debris and boulders—the flotsam and jetsam of a glacier. Those interested in the Ice Age will find not only an excellent variety of remains and records here—but glaciers also.

Hallett and Sprague glaciers, with their masses of greenish crevassed ice sliding slowly down their slopes, are worth long journeys to behold.

A mention of Wind River Canyon may suggest some of the delights that are stored in and around a score of other canyons and gulches. Down this gulch comes a clear, cool stream—leaping, sliding, splashing and reposing in fern-fringed pool. For a distance the stream will pass through grassy, flowery opens, then through an Aspen grove or Willow thicket, between high, rusty cliffs, and beneath beautiful, stately shining clumps of silver Spruce.

There is a wonderful fascination in scaling mountain peaks. The park mountains offer a variety of forms for those who, for pleasure, glory of learning, indulge in the gymnastics of mountain climbing.

Rugged Long's Peak is a perpetual challenge to those who go up to the sky on mountains—and there are not many peaks which require more effort from the climber; and few, indeed can reward him with so far-spreading or such a magnificent view.

The summer climate is cool and refreshing. It is an excellent place for the weak to get strong—or the weary to rest. To all, it offers strength, calm, hope, beauty and grandeur.

He who in Estes Park spends time by peak and stream, breathing the rosiny air, drinking the pure water—holding communion with nature—seeing the bright sun and the blue sky lingering over scenes and sunsets, listening in shadowy forests of the melodious tones of the Wood Thrush; or who feels a strong longing when the lonely moon gives light, mystery and shadow, or sleeps under the wide and starry sky—he who thus, for a time, enriches existence, will go away from its pictures to hate less, with existence extended—and life sweetened and intensified.

CHAPTER ONE
The First Settlers of The Circle

For ages the Estes Park and Rocky Mountain National Park region was a hunting and camping ground for the Native Americans. The tribes using most it were primarily the Arapahoe and the Cheyenne. Although they probably crossed this region at various seasons of the year, they appear to have used it most during summer and autumn. Here they camped, hunted, sought spiritual enlightenment and had an occasional battle. Apparently the liveliest battle took place between the Arapahoe and the Apache, in the western part of Beaver Park. There is an accumulation of stones here which probably is the ruins of the fortifications used in this battle.

There are some strange circles marked on rock and soil in Moraine Park that may interest you.

It is impossible to say who the first white visitor to this section was, but we know Kit Carson was here. He and a band of trappers appear to have trapped in Estes Park in 1840. Apparently they came in from the Poudre region and crossed southward to the Saint Vrain. Other trappers appear to have entered the Big Thompson Canyon even earlier than this, but turned back before the Park region was reached on account of the ruggedness of the canyon.

Kit Carson and another companion built a cabin on a little stream about half a mile from Long's Peak Inn. Here they appear to have trapped for a few months. The date of the building of this cabin was likely 1851, although it may have been two or three years later.

The first permanent settlement in the Estes Park region was made by Joel Estes in 1860. The Park was named in honor of its first settler. Joel Estes, like Boone, enjoyed being far from neighbors and wandered into Colorado from Arkansas. One autumn day in 1859, while hunting, he ascended Park Hill and from this vantage point had the wonderful view down into Estes Park. Early in 1860 Mr. and Mrs. Estes and their son, Milton, moved into the Park, with their effects upon two pack horses. They came in mostly "for hunting and prospecting." A log cabin was built on Willow Creek, about one block north of the "ranch house" near the junction of the Longmont and Loveland roads. In 1861 they brought in a two-wheeled cart.

When Estes first came to the Park he saw new lodge poles and other recent Native American signs, but, so far as known, no Native Americans have camped in the Park since the white man came. In the summer of 1860, in a gulch about one-half mile south of Mary Lake, Milton captured a black pony. Straggling arrow heads have since been found over the Park.

In the spring of 1861, Milton Estes, then twenty-one, journeyed to Fort Lupton and wedded Miss Mary L. Fleming, returning to the Park with his bride. Their son, Charles F. Estes, born February 19, 1865, was the first white child born in the Park.

The Estes families lived the simple life. Twice each year they went to the Denver post office for their mail. On these eventful trips, which were made during the spring and fall, they took a small quantity of fish, game or hides to market.

Reviewing her pioneer life, from the distance of forty years, Mrs. Milton Estes says: "We kept well, enjoyed the climate, had plenty of fun, were monarch of all we surveyed, had no taxes, and were contented as long as we remained—but I wish I had pictures of ourselves in those old days and clothes—how we must have looked!".

Several people who called upon the Esteses, while they were "monarch of all they surveyed," left written words of praise for their hospitality and jolly nature.

Mrs. Milton Estes not only had a cheerful disposition, but was an excellent cook and housekeeper. Every day at regular hours, she served three good meals. The ordinary meal consisted of venison, mutton, or trout; hot biscuits, butter, berries, coffee and plenty of cream. Cooking was done over the fireplace in kettles, pans, and in a dutch oven. Eagle wings oft-times served for brooms, and pitch pine in the fireplace generally furnished the light.

Sundays and holidays were scarcely noticed—every day was their best day. The Estes children had some pet cats and a dog, Mage, that caught fish. With sticks, rocks, sheep and elk horns for toys, the children spent their days happily.

One day little George Estes fell and dislocated his arm, but as doctors were out of the question, the children of the pioneers established the custom of keeping well— a custom still closely followed by Park children. The little folks wore dresses made from flour sacks, and all the children were proud of their buckskin moccasins.

One of the Estes children became a physician, another served in the Iowa legislature, and Charles F. Estes is at present working in Boulder, Colorado.

The Estes family were at home three years before the first visitors—some tourist campers—called. Among the campers who came in during the summer of 1865 were Rev. and Mrs. Richardson. Rev. Richardson was a Methodist, and one August day of this summer he preached in the Estes cabin to ten listeners.

Early in the winter of 1865-6 a deep snow fell over the Park and the entire winter continued cold and snowy. The Esteses began to long for warmer climes and scenes more remote, so early in the spring of 1866 they sold out and moved away. Joel Estes died in New Mexico, in1875; his wife in Iowa in 1882. Mr. and Mrs. Milton Estes, the past few years, have been dividing their time between their comfortable homes in Denver and El Paso, Texas.

The Estes families abdicated their scenic throne for one of the following considerations: Fifty dollars, a yearling steer, or a yoke of oxen. It is impossible to say which one of these is correct, but had Michael Hollenbeck given them all of these he had become a monarch dirt cheap.

A few months later a Mr. Jacobs gave $250 for the claim, but in a short time it was acquired by a regular Robinson Crusoe of a character called "Buckskin", Henry Farrar. Later in 1867 the Estes claim came under the control of Griff Evans, who founded the first permanent settlement by coming to stay. In due course it lost its identity by becoming some of the acres of the Earl of Dunraven. Evans remained at the Ranch house for twenty years as tenant.

Those who live pioneer lives are generally the most fortunate of people. They suffer from no dull existence. Each hour is full of progressive thought. Their lives are full of new occasions which call for actions that are accompanied with the explorer's charm—actions that make their lives strong, sincere and sweet. Their days are full of eagerness and repose. They work with happy hands. They are rich with hope and their future has all the promise of spring. To build a log cabin on the fresh wild mountain slope, and by its frontier fireplace explore the fairyland of enchanting thought, is indeed a blessing.

Early days in Estes Park gave a rare personality to its pioneers. Some of the good old people are still with us, and if you like the picturesque frontier restored with the concise vividness of early days, just lead any of these heroic old timers to become reminiscent.

The Chicago Tribune of August 15, 1871, had this communication:

"Mr. Evans and others contemplate putting up a cheap hotel for next season...I see no reason why this can not be made a prosperous resort, worth a dozen Saratogas to the invalid...But no one should come in a wagon, as a pony or mule is the best, allowing the trip to be made in a day from Longmont."

Prof F. V. Hayden, at the head of the United States Geological Survey, did some work in the Park in September, 1871. In his report for 1875, referring to Estes

Park, he says:

"Not only has nature amply supplied this valley with features of rare beauty and surroundings of admirable grandeur, but it has thus distributed them that the eye of an artist may rest with perfect satisfaction on the complete picture presented."

During the summer of 1868 Abner E. Sprague and two companions came to Estes Park on horseback and had an interesting and exciting outing. They had the good fortune to see the region when wild life was abundant, the trees uncut and the wild flowers at their best. Mr. Sprague returned in 1874 and climbed Long's Peak, and in 1875 settled in Moraine Park. He says the first land survey was in January, 1874.

In 1874, a stage line was established between the Park and Longmont. The same year Mr. and Mrs. A. Q. MacGregor came in and located in Black Canyon, where Mrs. MacGregor became postmaster the next year. In 1876 the post office was transferred to the "ranch house" and Mrs. Griff Evans became postmaster. John T. Cleave became postmaster during 1877 but did not move the office to the junction of Fall River with the Thompson, until ten years later.

In 1875 Henry Farrar built a cabin near the site of the present Presbyterian Church. During 1875, many settlers came to stay. John Hupp settled in Beaver Park; H. W. Ferguson at the Highlands; Rev. and Mrs. E. J. Lamb, after two weeks of chopping, got a wagon through to the present location of Long's Peak Inn; and Mr. and Mrs. W. E. James came to Black Canyon, but in 1877 moved and started Elkhorn Lodge. The Estes Park Hotel was built and opened in 1877.

On the 26th day of October, 1876, the first wedding occurred in the Park at the Ferguson homestead cabin, where Rev. Coffman pronounced the marriage ceremony for Miss Anna Ferguson and Mr. Richard Hubbell.

There is a sad incident of early settlement that came to a thrifty young German named George Bode. He homesteaded in the extreme north end of the Park, finished a cozy rustic home, completing the interior with striking wood carvings, then sent passage money to the dear girl he left behind. She refused the money, saying she would pay her own way, but desired him to meet her in New York. He went to meet her, but the vessel on which she sailed, with all on board, went down at sea.

In 1876 Israel Rowe, hunter, and the white discoverer of Gem Lake and Hallett Glacier, built a cabin near the home of F. W. Crocker, a short distance southwest of Mount Olympus. This year, Charles W. Dennison, who caused the first death in the Park, built a log house about midway between the cabins of Rowe and Evans. And this year, too, "Muggins"—George Hearst— pastured his cattle in Muggins Gulch on the Meadow Dale stock ranch. It may have been this year that the first flock of "hoofed locust"—sheep—were brought in. These sheep were corralled in a stockade each night, but this did not prevent mountain lions from leaping in and having fresh mutton regularly.

The first death in the Park seems to have been that of Charles D. Miller—for whom the Miller Fork was named. He was accidentally shot by Charles W. Dennison. The second death was that of a climber on Mount Olympus who accidentally shot himself. He was buried on the south side of Fall River.

The toll road from Lyons to the Park was completed in 1877, but in the nineties, after the charter of this road had expired, the company who owned the road managed, through some technicalities of the law, not only to continue charging toll, but to increase the charges. Efforts of Estes Park people to have toll charging stopped, or at least to have the charge reduced, were unsuccessful. J. E. Blair refused to pay and tore down the toll gate. He was arrested and fined. He tore the gate down again, and was joined by Abner E. Sprague. At the expense of several hundred dollars and much annoyance, these two men fought the battle to a legal finish. The toll company was defeated and these two men deserve the honor of giving Estes Park a free road.

The first public school was held in one of the cottages by Elkhorn Lodge in the winter of 1881.

Early in the eighties Mr. Cleave began to keep a few articles for sale.

Charles E. Lester registered at the old Long's Peak House, September 15, 1888, from South Hadley, Massachusetts. He went into the printing business in Denver and early in the nineties, was keeping a good little summer store, issued a very creditable advertising folder concerning Estes Park. He managed the Estes Park Hotel starting in 1893.

In 1886, F. H. Chapin, the Appalachian climber, first visited Estes Park, and during that summer, and the summer of 1888, he did much exploring on peak and in canyon adjacent to the Park. Many of his experiences around, and thoughts in connection with Estes Park, are delightfully told in *Mountaineering in Colorado.*

Shepherd N. Husted came to visit Mrs. John Cleave, his mother's sister in 1886. "Shep" made a trip back to Ohio, entirely on horseback. Returning to Estes, he fished and guided for the Estes Park Hotel and learned the carpenter trade from John Cleave, and later built his own home. During winters spent in Denver he met and married Clara G. Crawford; they were married in 1892 and took up their homestead in the north end of the Park in the fall of 1893. They built a number of cottages and took winter boarders; one of their boarders was H. C. Rogers, a London architect, who drew the plans for the Rustic Hotel, which Husted built and operated. Shep is a jovial guide and successful rancher, Mrs. Husted is a fine baker of home-made bread; she is also an expert with horses and says Lou Hubbell taught her to drive a team of four horses, when riding back and forth on the stage to Lyons.

Reverend Albin and Mary (Grim) Griffith homesteaded in 1890 and went into the lumber business in 1909.

R. H. and Louise (Macdonald) Tallant and their two sons came to the Park in 1898 and settled at the head of Devil's Gulch.

The Denver papers tell that the first Fourth of July celebration in Estes Park was held in 1897. About one hundred and fifty people assembled near the post office to see the flag raised, to enjoy the basket dinner and listen to the orator of the day—Enos A. Mills.

Each and all of the early settlers had many strange and interesting experiences—the alert and character building experiences of the pioneer. They had hard work, inconveniences, and occasionally hard times, but they did not crave sympathy–they were enjoying life.

CHAPTER TWO
The Earl of Dunraven

By 1867 many of the English tongue who were interested in scenery, trout, bison, elk, beaver or stock raising, were repeating agreeable stories concerning Estes Park. For five years hunters, tourists, trappers and homeseekers came and went.

Windham Thomas Wyndham-Quin was born February 12, 1841, from Adair Manor on the River Shannon, County Limerick, Ireland. He married the daughter of Lord Charles Lenox Kerr in 1869, they had one daughter, Lady Ardee. He inherited the title of Earl of Dunraven, substantial properties and wealth when his father died in 1871.

In the autumn and early winter of 1869, and again in1872, the Earl of Dunraven, with his guests, Sir William Cummings and Earl Fitzpatrick, shot big game in the Park. Dunraven was so delighted with the abundance of game and the beauty and grandeur of the scenes that he determined to have Estes Park as a private game preserve. His agent at once set to work to secure the land. Men were hired to file on claims, and ultimately about 15,000 acres were supposed to have been secured from the government.

In 1874, Albert Bierstadt, the celebrated artist, came in as guest of Dunraven, and at once selected sites for Dunraven's cottage and the Estes Park Hotel. Bierstadt was delighted with Estes Park, and made a second trip to it. Here he made sketches and secured material for some of his famous pictures. His favorite place was the shore of the lake which now bears his name. A painting of Long's Peak from Bierstadt Lake for years hung in the rotunda of the Capitol at Washington.

At this time Estes Park was unsurveyed government

land. Many of Dunraven's land claims were contested. His agent had secured much of the land by loose or fraudulent methods and some by bullying the home-seekers. A. Q. MacGregor, H. W. Ferguson and W. E. James contested the twenty-one original claims with the U. S. Land agent. The contestants claimed that "these twenty-one original claims had been entered by not more than five or six men; that the claimants had never lived on the land; that there was neither house nor fence—nor any improvements on any of the land." There are three "old timers" still living in the Park, who insist that the greater portion of Dunraven's land was fraudulently secured.

Dunraven came out with about 6,600 acres, but his agent claimed something like 15,000, and for many years controlled that amount.

Trouble concerning land titles and the rapid slaughter of game led Dunraven to give up the idea of a game park, so several hundred blooded Hereford cattle were brought in and his land was turned into a cattle ranch. For about twenty-five years these lands were used for pasturing cattle.

E. J. Lamb writes concerning Dunraven's last visit: he was accompanied "by his inamorata, who was registered as Mrs. Munroe, the celebrated actress of London, Dunraven presuming on American stupidity and credulity to hide the true facts of their connection."

An article in the St. Louis Post-Dispatch July 25, 1926 written by Ralph M. Coghlan:

"One day on the report of Abner Sprague, Dunraven and Mrs. Munroe were sitting at the long table at the Old English Hotel for Dinner. Joe Jefferson, the great actor, who had been attracted by the celebrity attending the Dunraven visits, entered the room. He knew Dunraven and he knew Mrs. Munroe but he sat down before he observed them together. When their relationship occurred to him, he arose and left the table to protest their presence in a hotel that housed his wife and children. Dunraven and his companion were promptly ejected from the Earl's own hotel, an incident which rankled for a long time."

With the second defeat of Dunraven's yacht, the *Valkyre*, in the contest for the America's cup; a ranch manager who was playing it fast and loose; and Dunraven's own extravagant demands, word became current that Dunraven would not again come to his ranch, and that the Hotel, livery barn and horses and 6,600 acres of land would be sold. In 1907, all the Dunraven holdings were purchased by F. O. Stanley and B. D. Sanborn. It is reported that to the new owners he stated, "I wish you luck of it. Estes Park has cost me a pretty penny."

From *The Great Divide* by Dunraven:

"Are we, I wonder really responsible creatures with our left hands knowing what our right hands do? Is there any continuity about us? How many contradictory feelings can we entertain at once? For years the idea of taking life has been repugnant to me, and yet I eat the flesh of slaughtered animals. To see the reproach in the dying eye of a deer would be intolerable to me now, and I could not shoot a woodcock or pheasant, or a rabbit, just for sport: and yet when I have a shooting party at home I am as keen as mustard, and long to have a gun. A mass of contradictions!"

CHAPTER THREE
"Rocky Mountain Jim"

James Nugent, "Rocky Mountain Jim", appears to have come to Estes Park in 1868, and built his cabin in Muggins Gulch, on the road from Estes Park to Lyons. His cabin stood at the mouth of the first gulch on the right as one descends Muggins Gulch. Jim's associates, his uncertain and irregular past, his braggadocio, bravery, chivalry, liking for poetry, and writing of doggerel, his debauches, moods, kind acts, his white mule, his picturesque dress, his romantic association with Miss Bird, the cowardly manner in which he was shot and his dramatic death–all these make him the star character who has thus far played in Estes Park scenes. Meddling parents with a lovely maiden in the background may have started him on his reckless way. He may have been "a nephew of General Beauregard" and hailed from the South, but he also claimed to have been the "son of an English army officer stationed in Canada." He seems to have served with both the Hudson Bay and American Fur companies, and to have bushwhacked in the Kansas "border warfare," and may have been with both Quantrell and Hamilton.

"'Rocky Mountain Jim' came down from Estes Park last Tuesday, bringing along 300 pounds of trout for a share of which he has our thanks. Jim never forgets a friend, nor an enemy, either."—Boulder News, November 14, 1873.

The Boulder News of October 17, 1873, contains this item:

"'Rocky Mountain Jim' is talking of writing a book. Jim has, under a rough crest, no mean abilities, coupled with a heart that beats right, and if he writes a book we predict it will not be tedious and unreadable."

It is known that Jim had a mass of written matter just before he was shot, but I have failed to find any of it. The refrain of one of his love ditties was—

"While in Muggins Gulch not far away,
Lived a poor trapper."

Jim hunted, trapped, kept a few cattle, and made frequent trips to Denver and Boulder. On a few of these trips he was drunk and quarrelsome, but generally he was jovial and generous. All old timers along the way between the Park and Denver with whom I have talked, say that they were "always glad to see Jim and his white mule coming."

July 6, 1869 he lost an eye and very nearly lost his life, in a fight with a bear in Middle Park. While creeping upon some deer, near Grand Lake, armed with only a revolver and knife, his dog came running up, closely pursued by a bear and her cubs. The bear at once turned on Jim, who fired four shots into her before she downed him; then with his knife he continued fighting until he became unconscious. He was lying in a pool of blood when he came to, and nearby was the dead bear. He was very weak and terribly "chawed up." His left arm was dislocated, his scalp nearly torn off, and one eye was missing. He crawled to his camp, mounted his faithful mule and started for Grand Lake. Twice he became unconscious and fell off. But each time, when he revived, the mule was found near by and remounting with great pain and difficulty, the journey was continued. At Grand Lake his yells for a time frightened the few settlers, who were expecting an Indian raid. When, at last, they ventured out and found Jim lying unconscious, one remarked: "Indians are 'round, sure; here is a man scalped."

Later, in Estes Park, Jim appeared to Miss Anna E. Dickinson in this light:

"...at 'Evans's', in front of a crackling wood fire, with time aplenty for confabulation, a confabulation that was made more 'pecooliar' by the presence of 'Rocky Mountain Jim,' who, having peregrinated up to see us, sat contentedly and looked at us with his one bright eye, finally in quaint language and with concise vividness narrating many a tale of bear and other desperate fights, one of which had two years before nearly ended his days–had broken his right arm, stove in three ribs, torn out his left eye, and 'chawed' him up generally, and yet left spirit and grit enough to tell a good story well and to get through a close shave bravely."

The lines that follow are a condensation of what Miss Bird wrote concerning Jim:

"Among the scrub not far from the track, was a rude, black log cabin; with smoke coming out of the roof and window. It looked like the den of a wild beast. The mud roof was covered with lynx, beaver and other skins laid out to dry, beaver paws were pinned out on the logs, a part of a carcass of a deer hung at one end of the cabin, a skinned beaver lay in front of a heap of peltry just within the door, and antlers of deer and old horseshoes lay about the den. The den was dense with smoke and very dark, littered with hay, old blankets, powder flasks, old books and magazines, and relics of all kinds. The owner, a broad, thick-set man about middle height, with an old cap on his head, with a hunting suit falling almost to pieces, a digger's scarf knotted about his waist, a knife in his belt and a revolver sticking out of his breast pocket of his coat. His face was remarkable. He was a man about forty-five and must have been strikingly handsome. He had large gray-blue eyes, deeply set, a handsome, aquiline nose, a very handsome mouth. His face was smooth-shaven except for a dense mustache and imperial. Tawny hair in thin, uncared-for curls, fell over his collar. Desperado was written in large letters all over him. He had no better seat to offer me than a log, but he offered it grateful unconsciousness. I read my letter, 'The Ascent of Long's Peak,' and was sincerely interested with the taste and acumen of his criticism on the style. He is a true child of nature; his eye brightened and his whole face became radiant, and at last tears rolled down his cheek, when I read the account of the glory of the sunrise. He then read us a very able paper on Spiritualism which he was writing. He told stories of his early youth, and of the great sorrow which had led him to embark on a lawless and desperate life. His voice trembled and tears rolled down his cheek. Essentially an actor, was he, I wonder, posing on the previous day in the attitude of desperate remorse, to impose upon my credulity or frighten me; or was it a genuine and unpremeditated outburst of passionate regret for the life which he had thrown away? I cannot tell, but I think it was the last...Yesterday a gentleman came who I thought was another stranger, strikingly handsome, well dressed and barely forty, with sixteen shining gold curls falling down his collar–the redoubtable desperado. Evans courteously pressed him to stay and dine with us, and he showed singular conversational dexterity in talking with the stranger, who was a well informed man. I left on Birdie, Evans riding with me as far as Nugents's. I should not have been able to leave if Mr. Nugent had not offered his services (to take her over the snow-drifted roads and ice-streams to near Loveland). Evans said I could be safer and better cared for with no one. He added: 'His heart is good and kind, as kind as ever beat. He's a great enemy of his own, but he's living pretty quietly for the last four years.' The two men (Evans and Jim) shook hands kindly. Some months later 'Rocky Mountain Jim' fell by Evans own hand–shot from Evans' doorstep while riding past his cabin."

Evans was drunk when he shot Jim. The stories that Jim was in love with Evans' daughter, and that he insulted her, are stories that seem not to have become known until after the shooting. Evans and Jim were incompatible; both drank heavily at times, and they had several quarrels. Evans was associated with those who were scheming to secure fraudulently the whole of Estes Park for Lord Dunraven. Jim opposed his land scheme, and opposed it with threatening armed presence, and his pen. At the time that Jim was shot he seemed to be making a winning fight against the land scheme. Naturally the old-timers were with Jim, and a consensus of their opinions is that "English gold killed Jim for opposing the land scheme."

Evans told the writer that he shot Jim for insulting his daughter. But incidental remarks of Evans to the writer concerning the affair did not harmonize with the studied assertion. A claim is made that there was a woman in the case; a woman to whom Dunraven and Jim were both paying attention. The common belief of the neighbor-hood at the time of the shooting was that "Evans was hired to do it." It does seem that Evans was only an agent when he did the shooting, but his hatred for Jim and the hatred of his backer, the land unpleasantry and the whisky all combined in causing Evans to do the shooting.

A friend, by the name of Brown, who was with Jim at the time of the shooting, gave Abner E. Sprague an account of it a day or two after it happened. Here is the substance of it: Jim and a friend were returning from a ride and stopped to water their horses at the little stream by Evans' house. Evans and Dunraven were in one of Evans cabins drinking—possibly Evans was being toned up to the deed. When Jim left the stream Dunraven, putting a double-barrel shotgun into Evans hands, said: "I want you to protect me." Evans took the gun, and as Jim passed near, fired two shots in rapid succession, and without warning. The first shot missed Jim and hit an old stage coach that stood by; but Jim, as the result of the second shot fell from his horse with a load of buckshot in his body. At the trial one witness swore that Dunraven said to Evans: "Give him another; he's not dead yet."

This fellow, Brown, disappeared a few days after the shooting and has never been heard of since. It is probable that Lord Dunraven paid this important witness to disappear.

For a time it seemed that Jim would recover. He wrote an account of the shooting for a Fort Collins paper, and in this he stated that the land troubles were at the bottom of the shooting. Meanwhile Evans visited Jim and asked to be forgiven; Jim's reply is said to have been: "No, damn you, I'll forgive you with lead when I get well." Jim did not get well and the talk of the time was that the attending physician was hired to put him out of the way. Possibly public opinion was correct, but it appears more probable "that a piece of buckshot that had lodged in Jim's skull had dropped in upon his brain," or that "the base of Jim's brain had become putrid from a piece of buckshot that had entered it the day of the shooting."

Mrs. Griffith Evans asked me to say for her that while she regretted the killing of Rocky Mountain Jim, she could not blame her husband for the deed as it appeared to be a case of kill or be killed. At times Jim drank heavily and when drinking he frequently was quarrelsome. Both when he was drunk and when he was sober he had repeatedly threatened to kill Evans.

From *Past Times and Pastimes* by Dunraven:

"Estes Park was inhabited by a little Welshman—Evans, who made a living I don't know how and by Mountain Jim, who trapped—an extraordinary character, civil enough when sober, but when drunk, which was as often as he could manage, violent and abusive, and given to declamation in Greek and Latin. Evans lived in quite a decent, comfortable log-house, and Jim in a shanty some fifteen miles away. Evans and Jim had a feud, as per usual about a woman—Evans' daughter. One fine day I was sitting by the fire, and Evans asleep on a sort of sofa, when someone rushed in shouting, 'Get up; here's Mountain Jim in the corral, and he is looking very ugly.' Up jumped Evans, grabbed a shot gun, and went out. A sort of duel eventuated, which ended in Jim getting all shot up with slugs; no casualties on our side. He was not dead, but refused to be carried into Evans' house. We carried him down to the creek, and fixed him up as well as we could, and he made a solemn declaration, as a man would presently be before his maker, that he had not begun the scrap, and that it was sheer murder. However he did not go before his Maker, and after awhile we got him back to his shanty. Dr. Kingsley went with him and reported that he could not possible live, for he had one bullet in his skull and his brains were oozing out, and he did not know how many slugs were embedded in various parts of his person."

This was the most serious Estes Park tragedy.

CHAPTER FOUR
Miss Isabella L. Bird

Early in October, 1873, Long's Peak was climbed by four people not unknown to fame. They were Miss Bird, ex-Mayor Platt Rogers of Denver, Judge S. S. Downer of Boulder and "Rocky Mountain Jim." In January, 1905, Mr. Rogers wrote for this book an account of his experiences in making the climb. The account pictures characters and portrays conditions in a masterly manner. Here is his sketch:

"In September, 1873, S. S. Downer (now Judge Downer of Boulder) and I rode across country from Greeley to Estes Park and we stopped for the night at Longmont.

"The proprietor of the hotel, learning our destination, asked that a lady, then at the hotel, might accompany us. We were not at all partial to such an arrangement as we were traveling light and free and the presence of a woman would naturally operate as a restraint upon our movements. However, we could not refuse, and we consoled ourselves with the hope that she would prove young, beautiful and vivacious. Our hopes were dispelled when in the morning, Miss Bird appeared, wearing bloomers, riding cowboy fashion, with a face and figure not corresponding to our ideals.

"Our progress was slow, as she rode a pony of no considerable speed, and it was well along in the afternoon when we came upon the cabin of Nugent, locally known as 'Rocky Mountain Jim', in Muggins' gulch. Jim came out and engaged us in conversation, his one eye, long hair and leather costume giving him a picturesque air—such an air as delights the romantic female heart.

"Miss Bird was interested, if not impressed, and when Jim gave her some beaver pads, which had been hanging against his cabin, she was quite ready to accept him at his own valuation. He rode with us part of the way into the Park and I observed then, as I did several times after, that in looking at his face from the side of his good eye, he came very near reproducing the conventional profile of Shakespeare. I forbore mentioning this resemblance to him as his vanity was already complete.

"The only habitable, if not the only inhabited, cabin in the Park at the time, was that of Griff Evans, and this was our destination. I can not speak of Griff without paying tribute to his genial, kindly nature, which it was my privilege to enjoy on several subsequent occasions.

"It was the last of September and the days were delicious. Except for the fence about the meadow in front of his cabin, the Park was untouched by the hand of the settler, and we were free to range it in every direction. Mountain sheep and other large game could be seen in the early morning coming down to water.

"We spent our time generally in riding with Griff along the streams and over the hills looking up his cattle—Miss Bird always being one of the party.

"Although it was very late in the season, she wanted to climb Long's Peak. She was continuously being reminded of experiences in the Sandwich Islands, and the event of her travels seemed to have been the ascent of the volcano of Kilauea. Now, the only guides to the peak in those days were Griff and Jim and each held in contempt and derision the trail used by the other in making the ascent. Miss Bird wanted Jim, and Mr. Downer was finally persuaded to ride over to Muggins' gulch and see him and make the necessary arrangement. Jim came, according to arrangement, riding a solid little pony and followed by his dog, Ring. Griff rendered us great assistance by cautioning Downer and me to keep our whiskey flasks from Jim, whose worthlessness in the presence of liquor was well known to him.

"We started early in the day and made camp at timberline, just opposite a tremendous snowbank on the slope of the peak. We spend the evening before the campfire, very much after the manner described in her book. Jim was resourceful, romantic and reminiscent. His adventure with the bear in Middle Park, which cost him his eye, was elaborated for Miss Bird's benefit, and all the doggerel which he had composed in the loneliness of Muggins' gulch was recited by him. The principal theme of his poems was himself, varied by references to a fair maiden, of whom he seemed to be enamored, and whom, we afterwards learned, was Griff Evans' daughter.

"We were up before sunrise the next morning. Miss Bird mounted her pony and the rest walked. When we reached the lava beds she could ride no further and her horse was lariated. After passing through the notch[2] Downer and I had a controversy with Jim as to the best way to get over the slide. He insisted on going to the bottom near the head waters of the Big Thompson, and then climbing again until Keyhole was reached. Downer and I thought we could reach the Keyhole directly and without the long descent and arduous climb. Miss Bird attached herself to Jim and we went our respective ways, Downer and I reaching Keyhole while Jim and Miss Bird were somewhere in the gulch below. This made a long wait, and when they finally came up with us she was so fagged that she was unable to make her way unaided up the last steep slope of the peak. By alternating pulling and pushing her and stimulating her with snow soaked with Jamaica ginger, we got her to the top. We were then so late that we could remain but a short time, and we started on our return in the early afternoon. Jim insisted on the miserable trail he had followed in coming, and consequently he and Miss Bird floundered in the depths of the gulch once more while Downer and I returned by the upper and more direct trail, which necessitated another wait on our parts at the lava beds. When Jim got her to the top again she was unable to mount her horse. She was therefore lifted on and practically held on until we got to camp, where she was lifted off, in fact, she was completely 'done'. We passed another night there and the following day returned to Griff's cabin.

"Miss Bird was quite taken with Jim, who represented himself as the son of an English army officer who had been stationed somewhere in Canada, and he made some pretensions to a former state of refinement. She was disposed to resent our want of faith in him and the jollying we felt compelled to give him.

---

[2] The lava beds are now Boulderfield; the notch, Keyhole; while the Keyhole here referred to is the top of the Trough.—Mills

-27-

"Downer and I looked upon her somewhat in the light of an encumbrance, though when her book was published we realized that we had had the great good fortune to travel with a woman whose ability to describe the manifold beauties of Estes Park has never been excelled. She was a thoroughly disciplined and observant traveler, although of too light a build to perform of her own strength the task she set before herself.

"Her physical unattractiveness, which so influenced us when we first met her, was really more than compensated for by a fluent and graphic pen, which made the mountains as romantic and beautiful as doubtless were her own thoughts."

She came into the park late in September and made her final leave in December. The Evans' and others say that, for a time, she was in love with Rocky Mountain Jim. Jim was a picturesque and interesting fellow and might easily delight a young lady author without her falling in love with him. She refused to write anything concerning her Estes Park experiences for this book. A number of things, however, would indicate that Miss Bird was deeply interested in Jim. During the closing years of her life she declined to write anything concerning the region and apparently avoided any discussion of it.

Concerning their final parting and the influence on Miss Bird of the news of Jim's death, her biographer, Anna M. Stoddard, says:

"Then they promised each other that after death, if it were permitted, the one would appear to the other. This parting gave her great pain but she felt that Mr. Nugent had undertaken to live a new life and that she could help him by prayer and her letters. Nearly a year had passed. Mr. Nugent's letters gave evidence of continued steadiness. Then suddenly on July 25, came the distressing news that he was dead . . . Miss Bird went to Switzerland full of the distressing conviction that Jim had died unrepentant and occupied with the remembrance of their mutual promise.

"From Hospenthal an almost immediate move was made to Interlaken and there one morning as she lay in bed half unnerved by the shock of his death and half expectant she saw Rocky Mountain Jim in his trapper's dress just as she had seen him last, standing in the middle of the room. He bowed low to her and vanished. Then one of her friends came into the room and she told her what had just occurred. When exact news of his death arrived its date coincided with that of the vision."

The following quotations from Miss Bird's book, give some of her experiences:

"A log cabin made of big hewn logs. The chinks should be filled with mud and lime, but these are wanting. The roof is formed of barked young spruce, then a layer of hay, and an outer coating of mud, nearly all flat. The floors are roughly boarded. The living room is about sixteen feet square, and has a rough stone chimney in which pine logs are always burning."

Of her landlord she wrote:

"Griff, as Evans is called, is short and small, is hospitable, careless, reckless, jolly, social, convivial, peppery, good-natured, nobody's enemy but his own—a jolly good fellow. His cheery laugh rings through the cabin from early morning, and is contagious, and when the rafters ring at night with songs, what would the chorus do without poor Griff's voice? . . . He has a most industrious wife, a girl of seventeen, and four children, all musical, but . . . though he is a kind husband, her lot as compared with her lord's is like that of a squaw . . . I pay $8 a week, which includes the unlimited use of a horse, when one can be found and caught . . . The regular household living and eating together at this time consists of a very intelligent and high-minded American couple, whose character, culture and refinement I should value anywhere; . . . a young Englishman . . . called the Earl; a miner prospecting for silver; a young man, the type of intellect, practical young America, whose health showed consumptive tendencies . . . is living a hunter's life here; a grown up niece of Evans; and a melancholy-looking hired man . . . We never get letters . . . unless someone rides to Longmont for them. Two or three novels and a copy of Out West are our literature. Our latest newspaper is seventeen days old. Conversation at the table: The latest grand aurora, the prospect of a snowstorm, track and sign of elk and grizzly, rumors of a bighorn herd near the lake, the canyon in which the Texas cattle were last seen, the merits of different rifles, the progress of two obvious love affairs, the probability of someone coming up from the plains with letters, Rocky Mountain Jim's latest mood or escapade, and the merits of his dog, Ring, as compared with those of Evans' dog, Plunk, are among the topics which are never abandoned or exhausted." — October 1873.

CHAPTER FIVE
Wild Life

Estes Park was abundantly stocked with game. Mountain sheep, deer, bear, lion and beaver were formerly plentiful, and elk roamed by the hundred. "It is a good thing we did not have modern guns," said Milton Estes, "or we would have had too much time on our hands." In 1871, while a boarder was eating breakfast at the Evans', the hired man asked Evans, "What shall I kill today; elk, deer or sheep?" Thousands of elk antlers were strewn over the Park up to the early nineties. Fortunately for the Park, mountain lions made early sheep ranging unprofitable. During the autumn of 1885 the manager of the Dunraven ranch offered $50 for the death of a stock-killing grizzly.

The Rocky Mountain News of September 26, 1896, contains the following:

"In Estes Park the usual routine of cards, drives, and dances was broken this week by the trapping of a bear. On last Sunday night a bear killed a steer belonging to Dr. James. This was discovered the following day and a gigantic steel bear trap set by the carcass and fastened to a small eighteen foot log. The next night the bear returned for a rare steak, plunged his foot into the trap, and dragged it and the log to which it was fastened, to a small lake near by. In the morning a few guests from Elkhorn Lodge visited the point of interest and found the bear sitting in the lake with his head covered in blood. The bear greeted his visitors so passionately that they flew down the mountain, never stopping until they met reinforcements. The party now consisted of about twenty-five men, women and children, armed with rifles and kodaks. Another advance was made, and a halt was not called until they were very near the bear, which was now on dry ground. Kodaks were aimed and the hands holding them were about as quiet as a seismograph in an earthquake. It was a case of shaking before taking, while taking, and after taking, too. The bear thought it was the pressing opportunity of his life, and charged the group. None belonged to the standing army. There was a stampede. Ladies and gentlemen trod on each other's heels; they tripped one another; they fell over logs in a confused manner and tore madly through the bushes. Miss James made a mistake and ran towards the bear. Discovering her mistake just as the bear was about to embrace his opportunity, she turned, caught her dress, and for a moment was in great danger. At last some one discovered that the bear had stopped. The stampeders stopped in order of lung capacity. The trap, chain and log had entangled among some aspens and held the bear fast. The bear weighed 800 pounds and measured eight feet from tip to tip."

The big animals are increasing and becoming more common. In 1913-14 the Estes Park people brought in a number of elk from Yellowstone. These and their descendants are frequently seen. Mountain sheep, deer and beaver are common. It is nothing unusual to photograph a wild sheep within thirty or forty feet. This increase of number and tameness is due to the cessation of hunting. For the past few years the people of Estes Park have discouraged shooting, and the National Park prohibits shooting within its boundaries.

Mary Lake, like Great Salt Lake, for many years has been slowly drying up, and about the only life in it are salamanders and axolotl—a link between fish and lizard.

Mary Lake, with its alkaline shore, has long been the Mecca for mountain sheep, and hundreds of these proud, graceful animals have been killed near it. As late as 1896, the writer saw young lambs, ewes, and old rams sporting, resting and posing on Sheep Rock and other promontories near the lake. Sheep still frequent this place. In the spring of 1903 an old ram became entangled by his horns in a wire fence just above the lake, and struggled until the barbs cut his throat so that he bled to death. It was a humiliating death for one of the proudest, boldest of animals.

Mountain lion and black bear are now exceedingly rare. It is possible that the grizzly still survives within the bounds of the National Park, but this is not positively known.

A numerous beaver population led trappers into this territory probably as early as 1841. By 1890 these animals were almost exterminated. About 1900, however, one or two local people commenced to urge beaver preservation. These primitive home builders are now on the increase. Beaver works, old and new, are found in a number of places; those in the Long's Peak valley, on the eastern slope of Long's Peak, in the western edge of Moraine Park and in Horseshoe Park are perhaps the most important.

Timberline is one of Nature's most interesting places. Here the storm king says this far and no further. The trees do not heed, but persistently try to go on, and the struggle for existence becomes deadly. The trees appear like our unfortunate brothers whom fate has chained in the slums. The trees try to stand erect and climb onward and upward, but in vain. The elements are relentless. The wind blows off their arms and cuts them up with flying sand. The cold dwarfs them, and for nine months in the year the snow tries to twist and crush the life out of them. Some live on as uncouth vines. Some become hunchbacks; others are broken, bent and half-flayed, while a few crouch behind the rocks. All beauty and nobleness of appearance is lost. But the trees have done their best.

Many beautiful flowers are found at timberline, along with bees, butterflies, birds, chipmunks and foxes. Timberline is a strangely interesting, thought-compelling place. Timberline is the forest frontier. Above it are alpine flower meadows, snow piles and crags. It is good to see it in the midday glare. It is a worthy camping place. A grand sunrise station and the place to see sunset splendors, the subtle charm of the afterglow and the palpitating whiteness of the "wide and starry sky."

Timberline is about 11,000 feet, and above it extend

fringes of Arctic willow. At timberline, dwarf and range pine, or white spruce, are generally found. A short distance below timberline the forest is dense and tall, and chiefly composed of Engelmann spruce. Mingling with the margin of these and draping some distance to the upper margin of red spruce at about 9,500 and yellow pine at 9,000, are lodge pole and Norway pine and a few Balsam fir. Most of the trees scattered over the park are yellow, black and white pine and red spruce, while along the streams are dwarf red and white birch and the tangling willow. Fall and Wind Rivers show many handsome silver spruce. There are straggling Colorado maples, a few dashes of sage brush, isolated rock-courting cedars, while the beautiful, graceful, legendary and gossipy aspens whisper everywhere.

Trees have tongues, and if you desire to interview a tree that has character and one which was growing when Columbus discovered America and one whose auto-biographic lines will give your constructive imagination nature history and tree poems, visit Old Artist, the big yellow pine at the turn of the road two vacation minutes south of the Estes Park Hotel.

While mountain climbing you may see an eagle on a crag or sailing far up in the blue. The American pipit and the Lukestickte are plentiful at high altitudes. Ptarmigan—Arctic quails—are found between 11,000 and 13,000 feet. Among the birds found below timberline are grouse, lark, thrush, blackbird, campbird, robin, Wilson wood-thrush, humming bird and the solitary and ever joyful water ousel.

Speckled and rainbow trout dart the streams. Among the other animals still to be seen are coyote, fox, mink, porcupine, cottontail and snowshoe rabbits. You will be entertained by that little monkey, the posing trick-playing, confiding cheering and dear little chipmunk. Then there is that wee and audacious bit of intensely interesting and animated life, the Douglass squirrel. He is alert, clean, wise, scolding, agile, brave, and conceit personified. He is an ancient woodman and plants many evergreen tree seeds each year.

It is illegal to kill mountain sheep or mountain quails—ptarmigan—at any time. There is a penalty awaiting one who rolls rocks or who leaves a camp fire unextinguished. There is only a higher law against pulling flowers up by the roots; but won't you help us enforce it?

Beautiful Estes Park is a fairyland of wild flowers. Ramble where you will or climb where you may, and the blossoms beam upon you. Nature strews each season with nearly a thousand varieties. The silver and blue columbine is found from June until late September. Orchids, pyrola, Linnaea, tiger lilies with "heart of fire," and the fringed blue gentian mingle their handsome beauty with multitudes of beautiful neighbors. Following the rains of early June, the park is colored and covered with blossoms. A petal seems to wave where every raindrop fell. The snowy mariposas and ruddy rattle-weeds sometimes show their color beds to the mountain climbers miles away.

The Wild Flowers of Estes Park
By William S. Cooper, Detroit, Michigan

"To the flower lover, or student of botany, Estes Park offers a wonderfully attractive field for study and enjoyment. In the park and its vicinity are deep evergreen forests, sunny meadows, streams with marshy banks, and, most interesting of all, the bare slopes and rugged cliffs of the range; and each of these different regions supports a flora of its own. The most important factors in the plant distribution are the climatic changes brought by difference in altitude. In the open meadows and scattering groves of yellow pine which cover the park is a plant with pea-shaped magenta flowers (one of the many species that are called loco-weed) which covers the ground in such profusion that whole acres are purpled with it. With this grow thousands of mariposa lilies, some white, others cream colored, while rarely a deep purple one may be found. Almost buried in the loose soil grows a small, globular cactus, with purple flowers, early in the summer.

"Along the willow-fringed streams are flowers in great variety, among them the shooting-star, monk's-hood, geranium, Indian paint-brush and the blue Mertensia, one of the most beautiful of Colorado's wild flowers. As we ascend the rocky slopes surrounding the valley, we meet new forms. In places on the mountain side is an underbrush composed of mountain maple, red currant, white flowered raspberry, and Edwinia, a shrub with waxy white flowers like those of garden syringa. The characteristic herbaceous plants are yellow stone crop, pulsatilla—anemone and fragrant white evening primrose which fades before noon. On somewhat exposed slopes may be found the blue flax and an occasional prickly pear, a straggler from the foothills.

"At an altitude of 9,000 feet are the famous blue columbine, the yellow pea, and Frasera, a freak among plants, which reminds one, with its thick spikes of whitish flowers rising from the ground, very much of a monument in a cemetery. The most interesting localities at this altitude are the mountain meadows. The Long's Peak Inn is located in a typical one of these. A stream with a sedgy border winds through it and Mertensia, marsh marigolds, pendicularis and Potentilla beautify its banks. The surrounding meadow land is a veritable garden filled with iris, larkspur, penstemon, and late in the year, with aster, goldenrod and fringed gentians.

"The region above timberline hold the treasures that are dearest to the flower lover, both on account of the bright colors of the blossoms and because of the small size of many of the plants. One must get down upon one's knees and search carefully over every foot of ground before he will find all the surprises that are in store for him. There are diminutive blue gentians less than half an inch in height, bellflowers hardly larger, and tiny alpine willows, barely raising their catkins above the surface of the ground. One of the most beautiful of these alpine flowers is the blue honeysuckle polemonium, somewhat larger than the plants just mentioned, but which grows at a greater altitude than almost any other. It flourishes on the very summit of Hague's Peak, at an elevation of 13,800 feet. There are innumerable others that might be mentioned, nearly as beautiful as this, and almost every shade and color is represented in these alpine gardens.

"Here in Estes Park there are new plants waiting to be discovered, and here a lover of plant life might spend many years and never exhaust the treasures of the park and its surrounding mountains."

Looking Southeast to Twin Sisters.
Trail Card Series Number 568.

Big Horn Sheep near Mary Lake.
Trail Card Series Number 652.

Looking West from the Base of Prospect Mountain.
Trail Card Series Number 264.

The Continental Divide.
Trail Card Series Number 318.

Kit Carson Cabin Site.
Trail Card Series Number 879.

Estes Valley from Twin Sisters.
Trail Card Series Number 382.

Estes Park from Olympus Mountain.
Trail Card Series Number J.

Mary Lake.
Trail Card Series Number 216.

Looking East toward Estes Valley.
Trail Card Series Number 444.

MACDONALD BOOKSHOP
PO BOX 900 - 152 E ELKHORN
ESTES, COLO. 80517
(970) 586-3450
www.macdonaldbookshop.com

B   38831 07/29/2018 12:33 PM

| 02945 | 1 ROCKY MOUNT | 8.95 | 8.95 |
| 18342 | 1 STORY OF EA | 13.95 | 13.95 |

	Tax:	1.93
CLERK	Total Due:	24.83
	Cash	25.00
	Cash	-0.17

FOLLOW US ON FACEBOOK!
ORDER ONLINE AT
MACDONALDBOOKSHOP.COM

Lone Pine and Long's Peak.
Trail Card Series Number 1081.

Estes Valley from Bierstadt Rock.

Big Thompson River and Road.
Trail Card Series Number 366.

CHAPTER SIX
Mountaineering

ALTITUDES

	Feet
Estes Park	7,500
Long's Peak	14,276
Hallett Glacier	13,000
Flattop	12,500
Hague's Peak	13,000
Lawn Lake	11,100
Timberline	11,000
Mount Meeker	14,000
Washington	13,100
Keyhole	13,000
Lily Lake	8,900
Park Hill	8,500

Though these figures are only approximate, they are within a few feet of the precise mark.

DISTANCES

For geographical reasons the Estes Park Post office is chosen as the basis for mileage distances, and the figures given are generally only approximate.

	Miles from Post office
Boulder-Greeley Colony	3
Thompson-The Canyon	3
Estes Park Hotel	3
Highlands	3
Gem Lake	4
Rock Dale Ranch	4
Wind River	4

Moraine Park Post Office 4
Wind River Lodge 5
Sprague's 5
Rustic Hotel 5
==Y Ranch 5
Horseshoe Park 5
Tallant's 5
Devil's Gulch 6
Cliff Dwellers' 6
Meadow Dale Ranch 6
South Fork 6
Lily Lake 6
Rev. E. J. Lamb 7
Horseshoe Falls 7
Long's Peak Inn 8
Twin Sisters 8
Bierstadt Lake 9
Bear Lake 10
Timberline (Flattop) 10
Timberline (Long's) 11
Flattop Summit 12
Lawn Lake 12
Glacier Gorge 12
Boulderfield 13
Hague's Peak 14
Keyhole 14
Long's Peak 15
Hallett Glacier 15
North St. Vrain 16
Allenspark 18
Lyons 22
Specimen Mountain 25
Grand Lake 26
Ward 30
Loveland 32
Boulder 33
Zimmerman's (Home) 33

Elkhorn Lodge, the stores, blacksmith shop and Telephone Central are all near the post office. The Estes Park stores supply everything that the camper can want or the tourist desire.

Estes Park is a real fairyland for children. It has plenty of green, clean grass for romping grounds; there are rocks round and square for playhouses, trees to climb, brooks for chip boats, thickets to explore, hillsides for racing and hilltops for geography. Children may be taken to the summit of Flattop, where are flower embroidered snow fields, and from which the little rivers start for the two oceans. There are here for the delight of the children, birds, bees, flowers, butterflies, and, dearest of all, wee merry chipmunks. There are willows, burros and ponies to ride. Estes Park is one of the most healthful and soul-shaping kindergartens in the world.

This, sir, or madam, is no place for ceremony or fine feathers. In Estes Park you will find all the wonderful wealth of nature that is suggested in the oft quoted couplet from "As You Like It," and it has more. Here are grander scenes than Shakespeare ever dreamed in his geography.

In all probability the first white woman on Long's Peak was the celebrated lecturer, Miss Anna E. Dickinson. Both Mr. and Mrs. Evans, who came to the Park one year before the first white men were on the Peak, and who lived in the Park for many years, are positive that Miss Dickinson was the first white woman on Long's. Miss Dickinson made the climb as the guest of Professor Hayden of the United States Geological Survey. The night after the climb the Hayden party camped at timberline, at the point touched by the present trail up Long's. While in this camp the party seem to have named the companion peaks—Mount Lady Washington, and Mount Meeker—of Long's. Miss Dickinson wrote the following concerning the evening's experiences by the timberline camp fire:

"We were taken in hand by the Hayden party, thereby gaining the experience and memory of Long's Peak, and the companionship through a few days of men who ought to be immortal if superhuman perseverance and courage are guarantees of immortality....I looked at all the little party, with ardent curiosity and imagination, braving rain, snow, sleet, hail, hunger, thirst, exposure, bitter nights, snowy climbs, dangers of death—sometimes a score on a single mountain—for the sake not of a so-called great cause, not in hot blood, but with still patience and unwearied energy for an abstract science—no more, since the majority can not work even for fame.

"We sat around the great camp fire that was kept heaped with whole trunks of dead trees, and watched the splendors of sun-setting till they were all gone, and, these vanished, sat on by the blazing fire by the solemn, stately majesties, talking of many things—strange stories of adventure in mountain and gorge, climbs through which a score of times life had been suspended simply on strength of fingers, nice poise on a hand ledge thrust out into eternity, wild tales of frontier struggles, intricacies of science, discussions of human life and experience in crowded cities, devotion and enthusiasm shown in any cause—all things, in fact, that touch the brain and soul, the heart and life, of mortals who really live, and do not merely exist. A talk worth climbing that height to have and hold."

Miss Katie Wamser climbed Long's Peak during a fierce storm. The day was probably the roughest that any climber had ever experienced on the peak. Miss Wamser, being throughly trained, enjoyed the day.

Miss Wamser, alone with the guide and writer, made a most trying and plucky climb through the storm to the top of Long's Peak. This was a remarkable climb as it required extraordinary nerve and endurance. Even the horses could not be forced to go above timberline, so from this place Miss Wamser proceeded on foot and several times was blown off her feet by the fury of the wind. From Keyhole up the rocks were dangerously icy, while the roaring wind flung cruel, cutting icy pellets and made the traversing of the narrow places extremely perilous. "At what point were you most frightened?" asked the guide of Miss Wamser as they sat resting in a sheltered place on the summit. "At the place where you appeared about to say we must turn back."

The best climbers are nor necessarily those who live in the mountains. The most nimble and sure-footed climber that has ever gone with me to the summit of Long's was Miss Elsie Bowman of New York. But she was no mere athlete. So entranced with the view was she on the summit that her lunch was neglected.

For good nature, lung capacity, endurance, alertness and skill as a climber, Miss Gladys Wells of Florida stands pre-eminent.

Two young people, with their chaperone, set off to climb Long's. I never did like chaperones and when this one gave out on the way up it was a delight on my part to be able to persuade the young people to go on without her. The chaperone called down upon my head the curse of all the gods at once.

It is dangerous for more than five climbers to be in a party on the Peak trail. A quarrel frequently occurs when there are more than five climbers, and sometimes when less. For safety, pleasure and enjoyment go with a small party. The scenes, altitude and effort on the Peak trail bring out intensity. The trail has caused friends of a life time to quarrel, and had broken "engagements." On the other hand, the trail has begun many courtships and time and distance considered, it probably is without a rival as a place for making "matches."

If one wants to go slowly and thoroughly enjoy everything, go with one or two companions of tastes similar to your own.

The park guides are unusually interesting and valuable. They know the trails, and some of the avenues of life, too. On an outing they show all a good time and are ready for any emergency. Shep N. Husted is a prince on the trail. Good natured Howard James has grown up with Estes Park for thirty years. Ed Andrews knows all about the birds and handles a kodak. Charles Chapman is a mechanical genius, and young Allison Chapman is a promising boy guide. E. J. Mills is a versatile choice of guides.

There is a three-story brick hotel in the wilds about thirty miles north of the post office. It is owned by an interesting pioneer who was born in Switzerland. Both the landlord, John Zimmerman, and the scenic trail to him are good to know.

One may ride to the summit of Flattop, where unfolds one of the grandest mountain views to be had in Colorado. The round trip can be made in a day from any of the hotels.

Olympus and Prospect mountains are worth while. They are not difficult; nor is Lily Mountain, on top of which you will find two wells in solid granite—dug by the elements. More difficult and delightful than these three is to view the landscape o'er from the summit of Twin Sisters. They are vigorous westerners and will entertain you with strenuous hospitality.

But something newer and more rugged are the peaks in the main range. Beginning with Meeker on the South and following around to Mummy on the North are a number of rugged peaks that have been but a few times scaled. They form the sky line that, from Greeley, Grace Greenwood said "loomed up more grandly than the Alps from the Lombardy plains." Most of their summits are above 13,000 feet, and to scale them you will have to go beyond the trail and traverse the untrodden places. Any of these trips will give you abundance of new nature stories, pictures and silences. If you still feel the call of the wild, cross over the summit—the Continental Divide— and explore the streamlets that are just starting on pictured journeys to the Pacific. Perhaps one of the easiest and most interesting wild trips is to cross over between Hague and Fairchild, afoot or horseback, and see what's on the other side of Ypsilon. From here you may follow down the streamlet to the wider waters of the meadow-margined Poudre, cross to the glacial and volcanic records around Specimen Mountain and return to Estes by the trail. After these trips among nature's statuary, manuscripts, pictures and powerful silences, you will not recite Thanatopsis so often, but you will feel it more deeply.

Every poet, geologist and glaciologist should see the Hallett Glacier. But in an ordinary season the trip should be postponed until late August or early September. Most of the summer is required for the removal of the winter mantle from the blue-green ice and the melting of the icy cement out of the crevasses. If you are to the manor born, you will want to visit the Sprague Glacier. It is not as imposing as the Hallett, but to me it is just as interesting; the scenes on the way even excel those on the trail to Hallett.

It is doubtful if there is another place in the Rockies where the records of the last glacier epoch can be so well studied. The remnants of the glaciers themselves are here, the records left on the polished walls are but little blurred and the embankments they left are but little eroded. Professor Kellogg of Stanford is writing an entire book concerning the glacial history of this section, and Professor Edward Orton, State Geologist of Ohio, has a lecture on the subject. Professor Orton regards the Mills Moraine, just east of Long's Peak, as the most interesting moraine, as it seems to show two epochs of ice activity. The big moraine by Moraine Park, and Bierstadt moraine, are studies. In Glacier Gorge the polished granite floors, glaciated walls, glacier lakes and ice sculptures—an abstract and brief chronicle of the Ice Age—is clearly recorded and eloquently told.

While perhaps not having the varied interest of the trip to the source of the Poudre and Specimen Mountain, the basin of North St. Vrain just south of Long's is wilder. It has moraines, forests, glacial meadows, beaver colonies, lakes, alpine meadows, cascades and a semicircle of bristling, snowy peaks.

Of the long, far-away trips, the one to Grand Lake excels. It takes you past Bierstadt Lake, gives a view into Glacier Gorge; Tyndall canyon is seen from the brink, Tyndall Glacier skirted and the top of Flattop reached. Here Chapin secured the photograph of Long's for the frontispiece of *Mountaineering*. This will give you a ride of several miles on the very roof of the continent. If you want to see a dead volcano with its beautiful crystals, geodes and fire-toned rocks, go to Specimen Mountain. There is much volcanic rock around Specimen mountain, but most of the peaks and crags are formed of granite and gneiss. Banded gneiss predominates, and many of the domes that rise above Fall River and Black Canyon display foliated granite. If you care to go further than this crater, a few miles further on, the Atlantic and Pacific ditch will interest as an irrigation enterprise. This ditch takes a stream from the Pacific slope and sends it home over the Atlantic slope. Just beyond rises Mount Richthofen—a peak for the climber. From here you descend the Pacific slope through wild alpine gardens and a splendid primeval forest to Grand Lake, one of the largest and imposing of Colorado's mountain lakes.

A horseback ride around the Circle not only shows the lovely and the wild in varied and ever changing scene, but it is a trip that the scene lover cannot afford to miss. Start from the post office; up Fall River to Horseshoe Park and Falls, then to Sprague's, Moraine Park, down to Wind river, double to Wind River Lodge, up the trail to Long's Peak Inn, then down past Lily and Mary lakes and the Estes Park Hotel to the Rustic, and then to the starting place—thirty-five miles. This can be done in a day, but should be enjoyed in deliberate installments.

Moraine Park should be seen for its moraines, flowers, pines, and for its view of Long's Peak and the range. The horseback ride to the pool, three miles west of Moraine Park will show one, nature statuary, swift water, glens and fern-trimmed granite walls.

The road along Fall River between the post office and Horseshoe Park is as artistic and aromatic as even a poet could desire. Horseshoe Park with its happy groupings of trees, sunny openings, running water and the grandeur of the sky-going range, will win the heart of any artist.

One of the grandest exhibitions of light and shadow and sunset's tints, gleams and sky lines may be seen centered around the Crags in the South end of the Park.

If you are in love with the Garden of the Gods and do not wish this love to grow cold, you would better avoid the lovely and romantic shores of Mary Lake.

Take your lunch some day and horseback into Devil's Gulch and see how inappropriately it was named.

The horseback ride to Lawn Lake is a grand one, and takes one up Black Canyon through the dark woods past the white lace of cascades, gives glimpses of cathedral rocks, past the neck of Mummy, to the lawn and tree trimmed shore of Lawn Lake. A short ride beyond this will carry one above timber-line to the rocky shore of Crystal Lake. Return by following Fall River through Horseshoe Park. This will show the appalling ruin that a forest fire brought to grand forest temples, some picturesque moraines, a beaver colony—house, dam and pond. On the right you will see the broken magnificence of Ypsilon and then pass into a narrow but lovely aspen avenue and emerge by Horseshoe Falls where Fall River in wild, glad energy dashes plunging, shouting, sliding, dodging in irised whiteness over the foam-flecked boulders among the fir and aspen trees. This cascading water is the boldest and most picturesquely broken of any wild cataract that I have ever seen "leap in glory."

Gem Lake is dainty and fascinating on the mountain top, and is not only unique but incomparably beautiful.

Chasm Lake has an utterly wild, awesome grandeur of its own. It is at the bottom of the east precipice on Long's, which is one of the great precipices of the world. From its broken shores the terribly shattered precipices of Long's, Washington and Meeker plunge up, up, far into the blue. In midsummer small icebergs float its surface as though it were a miniature Arctic ocean and the few flowers, birds and animals on its shores may almost all be found on the faraway Arctic Circle. Coming down to the lake from the summits above is a large, winding snow and ice field that meets the requirements of a glacier. Below it the Mills Moraine winds away with its enormous and bouldered sides, telling the stories of two ice epochs.

Chapin, in speaking of Long's and Estes Park, says: "I would not fail to impress on the mind of the tourist that the scenes are too grand for words to convey a true idea of their magnificence. Let him, then, not fail to visit them." Of Chasm lake Chapin says: "Taken in conjunction with the view of the tower of Long's Peak, rising 3,000 feet above the observer, and exposing a grand slope, few sublimer sights can be met with in the chain of the Rockies."

AWFUL NIGHT IN A BLIZZARD
Lost Above Timberline Four Men and a Woman Are Forced to Camp Without Fire in Cleft of Rocks for Shelter from Terrible Storm

"Estes Park, Colo, Sept. 23, 1896.–The storm of Saturday and Sunday was a raging blizzard on Flattop trail, between Middle Park and Estes Park, and a party of four men and a woman, after losing the trail was compelled to spend the night above timberline, without a fire, and huddled together for shelter into a cleft in the rocks.

"F.P. Wolaver, A.W. Locke, Mr. and Mrs. A. E. Sprague and James Cairns, started with their pack outfit from Grand Lake to Estes Park. They camped just below timberline on the west side of Flattop one evening, intending to cross over the next day. There were gusts of wind, glimpses of the moon between flying clouds, and finally a light fall of snow during the night.

"The morning was wintry, a poor one for trailing on the heights. Clouds were low and were swiftly flying across the range from west to east. Snow above timberline was whirling and drifting. But the campers were anxious to cross, and occasional glimpses of the sun in the wintry sky, as they breakfasted, gave some promise of clearing weather. So they packed up and started. Three of the party were tenderfeet. Shortly the snow began falling thick and fast, and as they reached timberline they climbed up into the clouds. It was cold, damp and dark. Mr. Sprague, who had been over the trail in all kinds of weather, led the way. The trail was steep and slippery, and the summit some distance away. For a moment the clouds were broken and parted, and then they closed in again. It began to blow harder, but Mr. Sprague thought he could keep his bearings, so on they went. They were traveling with the storm. It began to snow harder, the wind became fiercer, the storm increased every minute. It was dangerous to go on, but it was impossible to return. Men could not, and stock would not, face such a storm. The trail was obliterated. Mr. Sprague depended on steering with an angle of the wind to keep on the right course. As soon as the party reached higher ground the wind, less obstructed and deflected, blew from a few points south of west. This was then unknown. No word was spoken for some time. The storm was so thick it was impossible to see fifty feet in any direction. The animals were moving masses of snow and ice and were with difficulty kept together.

"Mr. Sprague could see nothing familiar, and told the party that he could not tell just where they were, and that the only thing to do was to keep moving and seek the first shelter.

"Suddenly a halt was called. They were on the brink of a precipice of unknown depth; the snow drifted over and disappeared. This precipice faced the south, and this told them they were too far to the left. But they could not face the storm and get back on the trail.

"So they drifted before the wind along the brink of the precipice, looking for some hole to crawl into. Mr Wolaver's hat blew off, and a handkerchief tied around his ears was soon covered with ice.

"After traveling for some distance along the brink of the precipice, they were stopped by a large mass of broken rock, which their animals could not cross. Thus cornered, all sought shelter behind rocks, from the fearful wind and drifting snow, but the snow would whip around and dash all over them. All were soon terribly chilled. Here Mr. Sprague found a shelf on the edge of a cliff. Here the wind could not strike, and all could breathe freely. In looking around they discovered a cleft in the wall of the precipice. This cleft was about twenty feet below the top, and was about eight feet long by six feet wide. They decided to occupy it. Mrs. Sprague was lowered into this with a rope, then the bedding and supplies lowered to her. A tepee tent was last lowered, the rope was tied to the top of this, then made fast to the rocks above. All squeezed into the tent and sat down on the bedding. It was 1:30 p.m. They tried to eat their dry, cold lunch, but they had no water, and could not eat without it. They could hear only the fiercer blasts and the sifting of the snow on the tent.

"A few minutes past two o'clock the eastern sky cleared a little. The snow almost ceased, and the wind went down. They decided to leave and try for the trail. They hurriedly packed and hustled out of the cleft, and were just making a start, when the storm came on with greater fury than ever and drove them back to the cleft for refuge for the night. Such a refuge! A hole in a cold rock, into which they could all barely squeeze, far above timberline, without fire, and a blizzard raging. A slip, or if a slide of snow struck them, headlong they would fall for a thousand feet. They were between a blizzard and a deep precipice!

"It was now 5:30 p.m. They ate a few mouthfuls of dry lunch. Their clothing was a sheet of ice. They wound blankets around themselves and prepared to dry their clothing with bodily heat. With much crowding and squeezing they managed to get into something of a reclining position, all forming a big wedge with all feet in a pile at the small end.

"A miserable, slow-going night was spent; cramps, cat-naps and reflection!

"At last the fires of sunrise gladdened all. The birds began to twitter along the cliff and the bell on the lead donkey was heard tinkling above. Only one could move at a time but at last all got into frozen boots. Once out on top again they found the temperature warmer, but the storm was still severe. But to live they must leave the place. To move with the pack outfit was impossible. The only thing to do was to try to reach timberline on foot. With this idea they started, taking only a small pack of eatables, a pair of blankets and a rope for descending ledges. Leaving the animals to their fate, they worked their way along the face of the cliff, hoping they could find some gorge or gully by which they could descend to timber. They were facing the storm at an angle of forty-five degrees, traveling in the order of wild geese, the strongest in the lead, with pellets of snow driven by the wind, stinging their faces. At last they found a break and started down a trough in the cliff. It was very steep and filled with loose stones. They had to keep closely together, on account of danger from dislodged stones, which from time to time went bounding swiftly, dangerously far below. They slipped, slid and crawled, for an exciting and exhausting hour—when timberline, wood and shelter, was gained.

"This walking was a severe strain on Mr. Wolaver. He was sixty-seven years old, and accustomed to walking only in Lincoln Park and besides he was slightly crippled with an injured leg. During the night he had lain on the shovel, accidently left beneath the bed. This had not helped his leg. To make matters worse, while all rested at timberline, he quenched thirty-six hours of thirst with ice water, which sickened him. When all started forward again he had nothing in him but grit—but plenty of that.

"They were headed for Moraine, and, leaving the remainder of the party climbing over logs and breaking their way through the brush, Mr. Cairns and Mr. Locke hurried to procure horses and a wagon to send back for the stragglers at a point were they would emerge from the woods into the trail.

"That night, by cheerful fireside, friends and relatives eagerly listened to their stirring story."

In February, 1899, two trappers on Grand River ran out of provisions and started across the range for Estes Park. On the snowy summit they became almost snowblind, but managed to make their way down Horseshoe Park, where by accident they ran against a deserted cabin in which they spent the night. The next morning one was totally blind and the other very nearly so. Being unable to keep on the road, they followed Fall River. After hours of difficulty and danger they were attracted to the Hondius ranch by the barking of a dog.

In February, 1903, while snow shoeing across Flattop on the way to Grand Lake, the writer, in the midst of a blinding storm, walked out upon a snow cornice which overhung a precipice. The cornice caved off, but the writer managed to catch upon the narrow ledge just under the top of the precipice. He went on to Grand Lake where he arrived at midnight. The experience is described under "The Colorado Snow Observer" in *Wild Life on the Rockies.*

Another winter a trapper from Grand River lost his way on Flattop during a storm and barely escaped with his life, after a perilous climb down the precipitous icy walls of Moraine Park. He spent a night in the woods where his hands and feet were badly frozen, and the next day finally reached the home of Mrs. Arah Chapman.

In 1906, Miss M. V. Brougham had a strenuous experience on Long's Peak. She climbed it without guide or companion, except "Scotch," a collie dog and friend of the writer's. Coming down from the summit she missed the trail and spent a cold, windy night among the crags beyond Keyhole at an altitude of 13,000 feet. Scotch knew the way and would have led her home, but she declined to follow him. Fortunately he stayed with her. She hugged him all night but was badly chilled when the guides found her the following morning.

The Native Americans had a number of trails across the Range. The one across Flattop was known as the "Big Trail," the one by Windy Gulch as the "Child's Trail." They named many of the peaks, mountains and streams, and a number of these names are exceedingly descriptive and fitting. Long's Peak and Mount Meeker were known as "The Two Guides," the Rabbit Ear Mountains with their eternal snows ever fronting eastward as the "No Summer

Mountains," Specimen Mountain as "Mountain Smokes," Old Man Mountain as "Sitting Man," Deer Mountain as "In Butte," Echo Mountain as "Pine Ridge," and Lily Mountain as "Beaver Lodge Mountain." Lily Lake was known as "Beaver Lodge Lake," Cabin Creek, immediately south of Long's Peak Inn, as "Lots of Beaver," the north fork of the Grand River was "Coyote Creek," and Grand Lake as "Big Lake." The Big Thompson River was called the "Pipe River," and Fall River, "Little Pipe."

CHAPTER SEVEN
Since 1900

HOW TO GET TO ESTES PARK

The park is a mountain valley seventy miles northwest of Denver, at an altitude of 7,500 feet above sea level, and may be reached by the following routes: with Denver for the point of departure, take the Burlington train to Lyons, then stage to the park. Or take the Colorado & Southern route to Loveland, and stage the Thompson Canyon to the park. If one has a private conveyance, the railroad may be left at Boulder, and the park made via Jamestown and Allenspark. Or one may take the Switzerland Trail to Ward and then in private conveyance travel for miles parallel with the snowy range into the park. Of these routes, the Lyons one is shorter and the Loveland one the most scenic. The park is a scenic sanitarium. It is an ideal place to throw off care or to dislodge rust or disease. It is a grand place to meet your commercial rival beneath the pine tree's flag of truce. It is a great place to be yourself, to learn the sterling worth of others and to really appreciate the Nature World Beautiful.

Stay late if you can. September and October are the Park's best days. They have fewer storms and more even temperature than the other months. Do not be afraid of being snowed in. Snow is not often deep enough for the winter residents to have a sleigh ride.

Fortunate is the visitor who can linger into autumn. In September the grass comes out in tan, the willows in red, while the maples burst into flame and the aspens are pure gold. There is a quietude over all. Everywhere is rich repose. The hours are clear and calm and in the golden

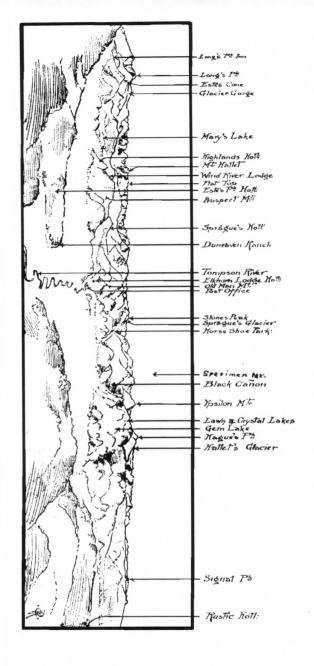

Long's Pt Inn
Long's Pk
Estes Cone
Glacier Gorge

Mary's Lake

Highlands Hotl
Mt Hallet
Wind River Lodge
Flat Top
Estes Pk Hotl
Prospect Mt.

Sprague's Hotl

Dunraven Ranch

Tompson River
Elkhorn Lodge Hotl
Old Mans Mt.
Post Office

Stones Peak
Sprague's Glacier
Horse Shoe Park

Specimen Mt.
Black Cañon

Ypsilon Mt.

Lawn & Crystal Lakes
Gem Lake
Hague's Pk
Hallet's Glacier

Signal Pk

Rustic Hotl

peace of the autumn days the flowers fade one by one.

The winter climate will favorably compare with Denver or Chicago. Zero weather is uncommon and of short duration. The park occasionally feels the breath of the Chinook. Nature does not give her best climate to the tourist months, nor do the home people of the Park expose their best nature to the throngs of summer.

Winter brings rest and happy days to the people of the Park. Sometimes they sleep later than the laziest tourist. Some go East on visits, or take their children out to school. Some turn tourist and visit palm lands. All make some preparation for next season's travel and give time to some good book.

The long distance telephone line first connected the Park with the outside world in 1900.

During the winter of 1900 a summer store kept by W. T. Parke, became an all the year round store.

Early in the summer of 1900 a man, in burning some logs out of a trail on the eastern slope of Long's Peak, neglected the fire and it spread and killed more than a thousand acres of beautiful, valuable forest. During the same summer some campers left their camp fire burning when they departed and it wrought havoc among the forests on the South Fork and along the Flattop trail. Both fires resulted from inexcusable carelessness.

Sam and Sadie (Boyd) Service came to the Park in on vacation in 1902, and like so many others fell in love with it and decided to invest their lives and bought W. T. Parke's general store.

Mr. and Mrs. Robert MacCracken homesteaded near Mount Olympus, also in 1902.

During the summer of 1902, Wind River Lodge was built and opened, and Long's Peak Inn changed owners. This year and each year following has showed a marked increase in the Park population.

Ed Macdonald came to visit his sister, Mrs. R. H. Tallant in 1902, also visiting Mrs. Tallant was Jessica Chapin, a kindergarten teacher in Denver. A few years later they were married.

January 6, 1903, is the date of the windstorm that did some damage, and September 7, the date of some earthquake shocks which caused some confusion but no damage.

1904 saw the completion of the road along the Thompson River between the Park and Loveland. This is one of the most scenic roads in the state and was built largely through the efforts of C. H. Bond and F. P. Stover.

J. D. Stead became the owner of Sprague's in 1904.

In February, 1905, a six times a week mail service was commenced in place of the tri-weekly.

On August 2, 1905, Louis Levings, who, with George Black, was climbing down the face of Mt. Ypsilon, fell and was killed by the giving way of the rock to which he was holding.

THE HOTELS

Most of the hotels open in May or June, and usually close during September or October. Each hotel has its special scenes, peculiar advantages and an atmosphere of its own. Every hotel should be seen, and, if possible, a stay made at each. With the exception of Long's Peak Inn, which is at 9,000 feet, the hotels are located between 7,500 and 8,000 feet. There are three or four private houses that make lower rates than the hotels.

Name of House and Manager	Post office	Capacity	Weekly Rate
Elkhorn Lodge, Mrs. W. E. James & Sons	Estes Park	150	$12 to $21
The Dunraven, Guy LaCost	Estes Park	100	$12 to $17
The Highlands, H. D. Perdue	Estes Park	60	$8 to $12
Sprague's, J. D. Stead	Moraine Park	125	$8 to $15
The Rustic, Wm. G. Edwards	Estes Park	100	$12 to $20
Lake View,	Estes Park	30	$7 to $10
Long's Peak Inn, Enos A. Mills	Estes Park	45	$10 to $18
Wind River Lodge, Chester Woodward	Estes Park	75	$10 to $17

For years a number of people had vainly endeavored to acquire a lot in the neighborhood of the Estes Park post office. This was at last made possible by Mr. C. H. Bond, who acquired a laid out townsite. The first lots were sold in the fall of 1905. The townsite was purchased from John T. Cleave, the best known of the old timers. He was an honest but eccentric Englishman who came to the Park in the early seventies and was postmaster for thirty years.

In June, 1906, the old Long's Peak Inn burned. It was

at once replaced by the present rustic structure.

In September, 1906, the Estes Park Protective and Improvement Association was formed with Mr. F.O. Stanley as President and Mr. C. H. Bond as Secretary. Most property owners at once became members.

Statements and Stipulations of the Estes Park Protective and Improvement Association

Adopted
September 22, 1906

Estes Park, Colorado
September 22, 1906

We the undersigned, residents or owners or agents of property, in Estes Park, Larimer County, Colorado, being desirous of Associating ourselves for Social purposes, and for furthering the beautifying of said Park, and not for pecuniary profit, do hereby associate ourselves together, under the following Statements and Stipulations.

First.
The name of our Society shall be The Estes Park Protective and Improvement Association.

Second.
The particular business and object for which our said Association is formed, shall be to promote Social intercourse among ourselves, and to suggest, provide for, and maintain improvements, such as roads, trails, fish hatcheries, tree planting, forestry, and any like attempts intended to be of use and benefit to the members of this Association and its associates.

Third.
The affairs of the Association are entrusted to Eleven (11) directors, who are herein designated as the Board of Directors. A majority of such board, shall constitute a quorum.

Fourth.

There shall be an Annual meeting of the Association at the School House on the second Saturday in September, at 2 o'clock. A majority of the members shall constitute a quorum—if there be no quorum, the presiding officer shall adjourn the meeting from time to time, until a quorum shall be had, and notice of every such adjournment shall be sent to the members address, left with the Secretary. If no address is so left, it shall be considered sufficient if such notices are sent through the Post Office. The order of business shall be substantially, as follows:

1st—Roll Call.
2nd—Reading of Minutes of last Meeting.
3rd—Reports of Standing Committees.
4th—General Business
5th—Election of Officers.

Fifth.

At the annual meeting of the Association on the second Saturday in September, the Club shall ballot for eleven (11) directors, to serve for the ensuing year. Whenever a vacancy occurs, in the Board, the Board shall have power to elect a member to serve as director until the next annual meeting.

The Board shall as soon as may be after each annual meeting, elect from its own body, a President, Vice President, Secretary and Treasurer, who shall hold office for one year, and until their successors are elected and accept office.

There shall be an Executive Committee, consisting of the President and three (3) directors, who shall be appointed by the Board, and hold office during its pleasure.

The Board shall have knowledge of, and determine all matters affecting the welfare of the Association, shall authorize and control all expenditures; ballot for candidates for admission to membership, and act as a court before which all questions or differences which might affect the interests of the Association may be brought.

The Board shall hold monthly meetings, and whenever it may be summoned by the President. It shall have power by a vote of two-thirds of its members to remove or suspend any officer, and appoint one of its members, to discharge the duties of such officer so removed or suspended. Neglect on the part of any member of the Board to attend the meetings of the Board for two (2) successive months, without a satisfactory excuse to the Board, shall be deemed a resignation of his office. It shall have power by a vote of the majority of the board, to forfeit to membership and expel any member of this Association for any conduct which in its opinion is likely to endanger the welfare, character, or interests of the

Association.

Sixth.

The Executive Committee shall make all expenditures authorized by the Board, have a general supervision of the affairs of the Association, and report all its actions, at each meeting of the Board.

Seventh.

The President shall call, and preside at, all meetings of the Association or Board, and have a general supervision of all the affairs of the Association and shall be Ex-Officio Chairman of all Committees, and shall appoint all Committees, not otherwise provided for—and shall call any special meeting upon the written request of any three (3) members of the Board.

Eighth.

The Vice-President shall perform all the duties pertaining to the office of President, in case of the resignation, death, dismissal, or absence of the President.

Ninth.

The Treasurer shall have charge of all the funds and securities of the Association, keep a regular account thereof, subject to the investigation of the President or Executive Committee, and submit the same whenever so requested by the Board; he shall pay such orders as are drawn upon him by the Secretary and are authorized by the Board; he shall deposit all funds, as directed by the Board.

Tenth.

The Secretary shall collect all fees, dues, charges, and subscriptions; he shall pay all moneys collected over to the Treasurer; he shall pay such accounts as are authorized by the Board, or are approved by the President, or one of the Executive Committee, in an order upon the Treasurer: he shall have charge of all instruments in writing, except securities of the Association: he shall keep a record of the proceedings of the meetings of the Association and the Board and conduct the correspondence.

Eleventh.

No person shall be eligible to membership of this Association, unless he shall have attained the age of twenty-one (21) years. Applications for membership must be in writing addressed to the Secretary.

The annual dues shall be three dollars ($3.00), payable in advance on the first day of October in each year. New members shall pay dues at the same rate for the time after they shall be admitted, beginning with the month next succeeding their election by the majority of the Board. In case a member shall fail to pay an indebtedness to the Association, for a period of two (2) months after given notice to pay the same, he shall forfeit his membership, but may be reinstated within three (3) months after such forfeiture, by the unanimous vote at any meeting of the Board, provided all arrears are paid. Any member resigning, or in any manner ceasing to be a member, shall forfeit all interest in, or claim to, any property or privilege of the Association.

Twelfth.

No debt, beyond the actual funds in the hands of the Treasurer, shall be created.

Thirteenth.
RULES AND REGULATIONS.

No roads, trails, gates, or any means of entrance, into, upon, through or across private property shall be obtained by this Association, without the consent in writing, by the owner, or agent of such private property.

Whenever, at the written request of this Association, the owner or agent of private property, gives written consent to this Association for any means of entrance, into, upon, through or across his property, where and when such is not, in the owners opinion, to his personal advantage, the Association shall be required, at its own expense, to fence, gate, and safeguard in every way, to the satisfaction of said owner of agent, his surrounding and abutting grounds, in consideration of his extending the privilege of entering and passing through his grounds.

Whenever the owner or agent of private property petitions, in writing, to this Association for a road, trail, or any means of entrance, into, upon, through, or across his property, it is understood that same will be to his personal advantage, and he shall be required to share with the Association all expenses involved, as may be mutually agreed upon between him and the Association, provided his petition is accepted by the Association.

There shall be no Camping, Shooting, Picnicking, or Fishing, on any private property, without a written permission from the owner or agent of such property, filed with the Secretary of this Association, and any abuse of the privileges under such permission, in the opinion of the owner or agent of said property, will entitle him to at once revoke said permission.

Fires, removing timber, damage to trees, growing grass or crops, buildings, or any kind of property, trespass or nuisance of any nature, removing or defacing signs placed by the owner or agent on his private grounds, shall in each and every instance be considered as an abuse, and be deemed a sufficient cause for the owner or agent of said grounds to terminate any privileges he may have permitted.

It is hereby expressly understood and agreed by all the parties hereto, that any permission, in writing, to this Association, by any owner or agent of private property to enter into, upon, through or across his property by any means of a road, trail, gate or otherwise, is simple a privilege, temporary in its nature, and does not, in any sense, convey or establish a permanent right of way to the public, this Association, or any person, and he can at any time, as he sees fit, withdraw and revoke such privilege, and close any entrance to his property, without prejudice or loss to him, provided he notifies this Association, in writing, and repays said Association the cost of such entrance, road or trail, said cost having been filed in the records of the Association at the date incurred, and due consideration given him of condition of said work, at time of settlement.

The intent of the foregoing articles of agreement, is to place upon this Association the responsibility of policing, regulating and enforcing the proper use of privileges extended to it by owners or agents of private property, and upon the success of this Association in so doing at all times, depends the continuance of said privileges.

Fourteenth.

The Board of Directors of this Association shall have power from time to time to make prudential by-laws, for the government and management of its business, provided any such as may be made are not contrary to, nor change the intent or meaning of the foregoing agreement.

Fifteenth.

The reading and signing of this foregoing agreement, constitutes the requirement to become a member of this Association, and to qualify him to be a member.

Directly, as a result of the activities of this organization, a fish hatchery, which has placed several million young trout in our streams, was built and maintained. The High Line Drive and the Prospect Mountain trail are the work of the organization. One of the best things accomplished is a development of a sentiment that is protecting the big wild animals. This organization condemned those who killed game out of season and it even discouraged hunting or shooting at any time. As a result, both mountain sheep and deer have become more numerous and tamer, and are frequently seen delightfully near the roadsides.

The wild flower notice posted by this association produced happy results. It has been copied by many civic bodies all over the United States. With the hope that it may be further useful it is reproduced in full.

"You can help keep Estes Park a beautiful wild garden. Spare the Flowers! Thoughtless people are destroying the flowers by the roots or picking too many of them. Neither the roots nor the leafy stocks should be taken, and flowers, if taken, should be cut and not pulled. What do you want with an armful of flowers? Those who pull flowers up by the roots will be condemned by all worthy people, and also by The Estes Park Protective and Improvement Association."

During the winter of 1906-7, Mr. John Adams, idealist and the most original character in the Park, organized and presided over an entertainment society which met weekly. Parts of every program were excellent; often something was presented that was thought-filled, original and suggestive. These refreshing entertainments were given to crowded houses and their general atmosphere was that of a good country literary society.

In 1907 an automobile stage line was established between Estes Park and Loveland; another one over the Lyons road in 1909. The automobile caused the picturesque old stage coach, that was so cruel to horses, to be laid aside. At first the people of the Park were almost unanimously, and many even bitterly, opposed to the automobile. But it was speedy and comfortable and from the beginning it brought increasing numbers of people to the Park and consequently has added to the Park's prosperity and development.

In 1908 Ed and Jessica Macdonald with Ed's son from a former marriage went into business, advertising: "Dry goods, groceries, boots and shoes; for women, riding skirts, walking skirts, bloomers, hats and leggins to match"; and to this varied stock he added books.

Among the hotels recently established are the

Horseshoe Inn and Timberline in 1908; Moraine Lodge in 1910, and the Brinwood in 1911. However the Estes Park Hotel was destroyed by fire in 1911.

In 1910 the Western Conference of the Y.M.C.A. commenced extensive improvements upon the former Wind River Lodge property. The plan of the conference is to have conventions and to conduct a large summer school. The attendance has rapidly increased from the start. Many of the instructors and lecturers have been people of national and international reputation. Every indication is that the school will continue to grow and improve. In 1913 the Western Conference of Y.W.C.A. held a very successful session in these grounds.

In 1912 Charles and Edna Lester leased and later purchased the Rustic Hotel from the Husted's. An ad in the Estes Park Trail, 1913, says: "The golf links have been greatly improved...the livery furnishes good saddle and driving horses...the hotel dairy and farm provide the best of milk, cream, butter, eggs, and vegetables." The outstanding characteristics of the hotel are the homey atmosphere which Mrs. Lester creates, and the enthusiasm with which Mr. Lester plans trips for the guests and sometimes guides them.

While honeymooning in the Park, Clem and Alberta Yore decided not to leave.

The epoch-making event in the history of the Park was the coming of Mr. F. O. Stanley. With Mr. B. D. Sanborn he acquired the old Dunraven land holdings. Upon his part of the land Mr. Stanley at once commenced the building of the Stanley and the Stanley Manor hotels. A half million dollars was spent in buildings and their equipment. They were lighted with electricity and in them were installed the first electrical cooking plants.

The investment of a half million dollars in a modern hotel in the wilds twenty-five miles from a railroad startled the business world; it also gave the Park publicity far and wide and greatly hastened its development. This large and adventurous investment required nerve, good business sense, the capacity to see the recreation needs of the future and showed great confidence in the future of Estes Park. The Stanley was opened in 1909 and the Manor in 1910. Both are already on a good business basis.

The old Dunraven hotel, built in 1878 by the Earl of Dunraven on a site selected for it by Albert Bierstadt, the artist, burned in 1911. In 1913 the Rockdale hotel was built near Mary's Lake and this year, too, the Rustic hotel was enlarged and its name changed to Lester's.

A number of permanent residents and summer visitors are endeavoring to beautify the village. In this connection it is an interesting point that the village has never had any organized form of government and is still without a mayor or councilman.

There are now a number of automobile stage lines, one each from Boulder, Ward, Longmont-Lyons, Fort Collins, and two from Loveland.

Through the co-operation of the residents of Estes Park and Grand Lake a road was surveyed across the Continental Divide between these places, and work commenced upon it in 1912.

During 1913 a trail was opened into the magnificent Glacier Gorge, Loch Vale, region to the northwest of Long's Peak.

In the autumn of 1913 the Estes Park Woman's Club was organized. For years the ladies of the Park had been active in civic work. They helped to raise funds for the Fish Hatchery and for roads and trails. Just prior to the organization of the Club the ladies built the Deer Mountain Trail.

In December, 1913, from four to six feet of snow fell over the Estes Park region, as it did over the mountains of eastern Colorado. This was the deepest recorded snowfall at any given time. However, the coldest and most wintery winter indicated in the records of thirty years was the one of 1916-17.

Early in 1917 so-called winter sports were definitely introduced as a part of the outdoor interest of this region. It is probable that the idea of using Estes Park as a place of recreation in winter-time will be greatly developed. Let us hope that the idea will become permanent and general.

In 1909 the author commenced to urge that about six hundred square miles of the surrounding region be made the Estes National Park and Game Preserve. In September, 1909, a mass meeting of Estes Park People and a few outsiders, together with the members of the Estes Park Protective and Improvement Association, unanimously endorsed this project.

The proposition progressed from the start and the press of the country gave it extraordinary publicity. In this connection, Mr. J. Horace McFarland, President of the American Civic Association, visited the Park in May, 1910, and enthusiastically endorsed the measure. The name was changed to the Rocky Mountain National Park.

After seven years of effort, the Rocky Mountain National Park became a reality in January, 1915. The following September the park was officially dedicated. R. T. "Dixie" MacCracken was the first and only Ranger.

Early in 1917 Congress passed a bill adding the summits of the Twin Sisters and Deer Mountain, the Gem Lake Region, and other scenic territory of the Rocky Mountains to the National Park. Its area now embraces about 400 square miles.

During the season of 1916 nearly 100,000 guests came to the Rocky Mountain National Park Region. The majority of these came to the Estes Park side, although a goodly number arrived at Grand Lake. Among the guests in Estes Park were the Hon. and Mrs. Charles Evans Hughes.

No prominent locality has ever gained this prominence without the aggressive public-spirited work of one or more of its people. The live wire of this locality distinctly is Mr. C. H. Bond. Chiefly through his efforts came the High Drive Road, the road through the Big Thompson Canyon, the Estes Park Post Office, and the starting of the Fall River road, 1912, from Estes Park to Grand Lake.

Anyone who has helped in civic improvement, or

who has assisted in any public improvement, will realize that Mr. Bond had endless work, serious obstacles, and bitter opposition.

Among the individuals, and newspapers that distinctly helped to promote the National Park project were the Denver Post, Mrs. John D. Sherman, and especially George Horace Lorimer of the Saturday Evening Post.

The original industries of the region were cattle raising and lumber. Incidentally, hunting and trapping. The people whose interests were stock raising and lumbering did not want these disturbed by a travel industry. Usually they had a contempt for "The Tourist" or coldly tolerated him. Generally any change for the development of the region as a travel center has brought out lively opposition. For a time the plan to establish the Rocky Mountain National Park had almost unanimous local opposition.

The automobile, better mail service, the telephone and the increase of land owners all combined to make changes in the customs of the Park

The cosmopolitan character of most tourists have left a liberal and progressive feeling on the residents who represent all political beliefs and many religious ones, with Agnostics, Socialist and food cranks in addition. But all often meet for a union celebration and dinner.

The union dinners and entertainments are held in the school house and are the triumphs of cookery and joy. Everyone in the park comes with heaping basket and good nature overflowing. The school house becomes the storm centre of happiness and hospitality. The day is a blissful one for the numerous bachelors.

One old custom enjoyed by the early settlers was an annual public dinner. This commonly was given in the school house on Thanksgiving. Everyone was invited and a few far-off settlers came twenty miles. Occasionally, a Denver visitor or a straggling tourist was fortunate enough to be present. Generally there was some sort of a program in addition to the dinner. In effect, these dinners, like the old time log rollings, produced friendships and sympathetic, neighborly feeling; occasionally they promoted marriage.

The present winter population numbers 125, and from seven to sixteen scholars attend school. Sometime during the winter most everyone manages to combine business with pleasure for a few days in Denver. Estes Park winter homes are as hospitable as Scotch homes in the Highlands.

The mountains are imposing in winter. The splashing river is frozen. The leafless Aspens show their green-gray limbs in beautiful tracery, and the crags and peaks show soft and white. The wind often booms and roars through the pines where the picnickers shouted and snow drifts where the flowers bloomed, while sometimes the flitting, flushing Aurora adorns the dome where summer sunsets burned in glory.

If a poem worthy of Estes Park has been written I have not seen it. The following by the "Poet Laureate of Colorado," Mrs. H. L. Wason, would in autumn fit the park if the place was without its warmth of color:

"No narrow street shuts out the sky,
  No human throngs confuse our thought,
Our boundaries are mountain high,
  And these against the blue dome caught
While regal peace holds empire sweet
  To where the blue and prairie meet."

As I Remember Estes Park in 1916
by Esther Burnell Mills

Being asked when I came to Estes Park is a very unusual question, but in one case the reply was most unexpected: "I presume there were a few houses here then." It set me thinking, for it is good for the newer generation of both tourists and natives—as the local residents call themselves—to know that the past was not devoid of enterprising citizens whose lives were devoted to the growth and development of the region. Not only the town itself, but the surrounding area was well settled, as the saying goes. There were twenty hotels within a radius of ten miles from the town, six hotels at Grand Lake, and four shelter cabins that served people taking to the high country—Fern Lake Lodge, Forest Inn, Lawn Lake Lodge and Timberline Cabin on the Longs Peak trail. In addition there were hundreds of cabins for rent by the week, month or season; and the Y.M.C.A. Conference Camp provided accommodations for a large number attending conventions and conferences, and provided a variety of programs and activities for young and old.

I had not seen any railroad advertising or literature on Estes Park, but on the recommendation of friends, my sister Elizabeth and I had made a reservation at Lester's Hotel, four miles north of the town, and we were given the last available cabin—in the style of that day, half boards, half canvas. For people went to the mountains to rough it and enjoy the scenery. And such scenery! Probably the view of Long's Peak from this point is the finest in the Park area—the long, sloping meadows in the foreground seemed to set-off its grandeur to the best possible advantage.

Mr. and Mrs. Lester were ideal hosts, looking after each of their guests as though they were personal friends. Mr. Lester has been connected with Dunraven's "Old English Hotel" until its burning down in 1911, and knew the answers to all your questions about the region, with a broad sense of humor. He was also a wonderful guide, and his favorite trip with tenderfeet was to lead them a round-about way to Gem Lake, so that you came upon it as a complete surprise. He told the story of a woman who had been promised this trip and heard so much about it that they feared she might be disappointed when she saw the size of it, somewhat diminished by the end of the summer. Undaunted she replied, "Well, I think they did well to have a lake here at all." How true! The lake appears to have no inlet or outlet, having a solid rock basin, with rocky cliffs around it. The reflections which it holds magnify and glorify its size.

But what of the main street, only of later years dignified by the name of Elkhorn Avenue? The board sidewalks had doubtless been put in by each store-keeper, as they were not always on the same level or width, but they were reminiscent of our childhood days in Pleasant Hill, Tennessee, and seemed not at all out of place for a mountain town. Here and there were benches that provided sociability for the out-of-town visitors, during off-seasons when business was not too rushing.

The post office was in the building now occupied by the Town Hall, and Will Tallant was postmaster. Across from it was Grubb's Livery barn, a lively place any hour of the day, and no matter how much of a novice you might be, horseback riding was a necessity for reaching the points of interest beyond the town.

Foremost among the business establishments was Sam's Service's General Merchandise store, for not only did Mr. Service dispense groceries, hardware, feed and fuel, but was looked upon as the one most likely to have the latest news about any and every recent happening, in fact something of a daily newspaper. His heart was as large as his stock of goods, and his generosity to those who were just getting a toe-hold in the region, was unbound. The Service's home was next door to the store, and Mrs. Service could tend both home and store and raise a large family with the minimum of time lost. Two of the children still make their home in Estes, Rhoda Tallant who assists most ably in Macdonald's Bookstore and Mrs. Ted Scott, whose husband has been a post office employee for many years. Further up the street was the Pine Cone Hotel, operated by Mrs. Harriet Byerly, in same location as the <u>present</u> National Park Hotel—run by her son, Lee.

Then we had Parke's Photographic and souvenir store. Not only did he have a very large collection of photographs of the early days, but he gave help to tourists with their new-fangled kodaks which they did not know how to use.

The Hupp Hotel was located at it's present location, and Mrs. Josephine Hupp's dining-room was probably the most popular in town. For in the weeks that I was attempting to build a cabin on my homestead, three and one half miles from town, I was tramping back and forth each day and my appetite knew no bounds!

The Bank was doing a thriving business then as now, and seems to elude any competition in that field.

Further along the street was Fred Clatworthy's studio, and from Mr. Clatworthy's camera came some of the first color negatives. Mrs. Clatworthy and Helen still make their home in Estes Park.

The Community Church has held to the same location, even though some think it is occupying too valuable property for just a mere church. But sentiment is strong, and the church founders hold to tradition.

The Osborns lived beyond the church, where the Crowell home is now. Across the street, was the L.E. Grace Gift and Photo Shop. Mr. Grace was not only a fine photographer, but skilled in jewelry and silver work, a craftsman of the highest order. He was instrumental in helping the school organize a band securing the necessary instruments and uniforms.

Church's Confectionery was a general meeting place, and must have been the beginning of the "coffee break" custom, for at any hour of the day, and perhaps night, there was always coffee and a snack, or cold drinks, and an abundance of conversation with it. George Church did a thriving business in repairing boots and shoes, at a time when hiking was more general than at present, and his half-soles would out-wear the original many times over. Snow-shoes too, came in for some of his skill, as I can testify.

Dr. Roy Wiest was the only doctor in town, and with his wife operated the Estes Park Drug Store. On the corner where the Curio store is at present, was the National Park Hotel, run by Mr. and Mrs. Francis. He was a great nature-lover, and during the winter of 1917-1918 organized a Nature Study Club that met to discuss the latest observations of wild life and weather lore that develops from watching their habits and movements. He was a fine photographer and had many unusual beaver pictures. He later went into the photographic field exclusively, and had his store next to Grace's Gift Shop.

One of the very early establishments was Miss E. M. A. Foot's Dry Goods and Clothing Store, standing on the corner where Williamson's store is now. She carried everything from straw hats to golf socks but it varied little from year to year, for in that day we did not worry too much about the latest fad, and if you did not come with your own outing apparel, you might have to be content with men's trousers for horse-back riding. Whatever she didn't have, "just wasn't made." She must have had a shock when Eleanor Cohen came to Estes from Philadelphia, with tailored knickers with golf hose, and tailored coats to match, in a variety of colors, including white for Sundays and dress occasions! She further astonished the natives by walking all over the Park contentedly by herself.

Miss Fluta Ruple's store was like an old curiosity shop. It was about where the Plantation Restaurant is now. It occupied a small building, but the contents were enormous, the shelves reached to the ceiling, under the counter, and up and down through the middle of the store. It was a lovely haven for anyone looking for an odd button, a bit of lace or yarn, lap-robes, ear-muffs, gloves of every date and description, and whatever it was you wanted, she insisted if you would just give her time she could find it, and she did! Ready-to-wear, too, would be sold with instructions as to how a dress could be made larger or smaller, if your size wasn't in stock.

Ed Macdonald's grocery store was near-by, and how generous he was with the children who had pennies to spend for candy at recess-time—probably giving them three times the value of their money. Louise Macdonald Brown is one of the second generation of old-timers who has continued in business in Estes Park in summer. The Macdonald's home was next door, and along the same street were a number of other homes, being close to business, as well as the convenience of being near the stores and post office. Many of these families later moved up on the hill, which in time became the residential section.

Not overlooking the Realters, Mr. C. H. Bond had an office about where the present Bond Agency is located, and Hayden Brothers, Albert and Julian, occupied the building next to it, and were called upon for surveying as well as property deals.

The Plumbing business seems to have been entirely handled by Lindley and his son, Bob, who later took over the work. Bob's nephew, Maurice Rockwell became his successor.

The Estes Park Lumber Co., was in the same location as now, managed by Julius Schwarts. The Griffith Lumber Company also has stayed in one location, started by A. Griffith who homesteaded there, followed by his son Dan, and now Don, the third generation, is continuing in the business. There were a number of saw-mills in the region, to take care of the demand for log houses, but a great deal of finished lumber was brought up from towns on the plains.

There was only one garage as I recall, Preston's, located between Grubb's livery barn and the realty offices.

There must have been an ample supply of carpenters:

among them Fred Anderson, Elmer, Walter and Alva Jones, and M. Freburg are names that come to me, a few of the many.

The Denver Post of October, 1916 reports:

"Not since the mining boom days has there been such building activity in a Colorado town as now is evident in the Estes Park region. The rush of tourists to that resort last summer—utterly swamping every hotel, camp and private cottage—has led to a fever of building such as the Park never before has seen...Now that the "boom" is on in Estes Park, the more far-sighted of the residents of the place are working incessantly to bring about a general improvement in the style of building. In the front rank of these boosters is C. H. Bond, the man who for years has been the guiding genius of the region. In season and out Mr. Bond, virtually single-handed, has labored against old-fashioned ideas, apathy and selfishness to develop the right sort of a resort in Estes Park. He was the man who got the road built thru the Big Thompson canyon. He worked shoulder-to-shoulder with Enos A. Mills to get the Fall River road started. He started the townsite company and the water company and the sewer system. He interested many wealthy men from all parts of the United States in building fine, all-the-year-round homes in the park."

Probably one of the most valuable contributions made by the local people to the development of the region was in the field of guiding. Without these experienced guides the tourists would have missed many of the points of interest, and the enjoyment that comes from being with someone who knows and loves the region. Among these guides were Shep Husted, Warren Rutledge, the Higby's, Dolly Grey (when he was not busy painting and decorating homes).

Dixie (R. T.) MacCracken was the first National Park Ranger, serving from 1915-17, when he went into the service. His parents, Mr. and Mrs. Robert E. MacCracken homesteaded near Olympus Lodge in 1902, and the place is still the home of Mr. and Mrs. R. T. MacCracken. One of his first important jobs was to help build a telephone line from Estes Park to Grand Lake over Flattop. Later it was found impractical and was rebuilt over Fall River Pass.

Appreciation should be made of Mrs. C. H. Bond and her devoted work as Librarian, starting this in the school building until funds could be raised for the present Library Building. The Estes Park Women's Club sponsored this and maintained it through the years, with contributions from the local and summer residents. Her great interest was in having good books for children.

The first Winter Sports Outing was held in February 1917 at Fern Lake Lodge. The winter of 1916-17 was the longest and snowiest the park had seen, and those who had never snowshoed before, including myself, became quite adept. Fern Lake Lodge was designed more as a summer lodge than for winter use. Most of the windows had only canvas, and the airiness of our quarters made it desirable to retain our winter clothing for the night. The food that had been left for our use had of course frozen, and it was well towards midnight before the stove could be warmed up and the food thawed out. The bedrooms were decidedly chilly, and we stretched out on the floor to be as near the fireplace as possible, and whenever anyone got up to replenish the fire there was a howl from someone who was being stepped upon! Eventually, sheer exhaustion triumphed from the unaccustomed exercise that brought quiet, deep sleep.

An advertising booklet of the Union Pacific System "Rocky Mountain National Park, Estes Park, Colorado," circa 1920, mentions that 169,000 persons enjoyed these scenes in 1919. This is a beautifully illustrated booklet of 23 pages, that might well serve as a pattern of advertising for the Park today. It says further that the season is May 1 to November 1, but the Park is accessible throughout the year. I truly believe this should and could be the season, and even remain open throughout the year as the Conference Camp is so successfully doing. When so many services terminate with Labor Day or soon after, the morale of local people is lowered and they lose enthusiasm for seeing tourists come in. Moreover visitors catch the spirit of a gone-to-sleep town, and do not know if it is safe to stay overnight or not, lest they get snowed in. Get snowed in? I have only been marooned twice in the last forty-five years, once in April and once in October, for a few days only, when other parts of the country have fared much worse. Let's do a little adventuring on our own, and encourage our young people to do so, and the spirit will be contagious for all who come into this town, whether for an hour, a day or a week. There is no better scenery or weather anywhere, if one has the enthusiasm to get the most out of it.

A Tenderfoot's First Summer in the Rockies

by Flora J. R. T. Stanley, 1903

*Courtesy of the Stanley Museum of
Estes Park, Colorado, and Kingfield, Maine.*

Here and there in the rocky fortresses of the mountains, nature has let down, after the manner of Simon Peter's miraculous feeding—a sheet of verdure where bird and beast may find nourishment. Hither comes the hunter, slowly and singly at first, then in greater numbers, as the tide of population surges toward the mountains, until the hapless creatures of the chase are exterminated or driven to more inaccessible places.

The hunt for game and for gold has helped to open up these charming mountain retreats to the more gentle pursuits of enjoying nature and regaining health. After the discovery of gold in the West, every peak was suspected of holding in its grim grasp the precious metal, and every valley was mellowed with the miner's pick and shovel. The ranchman, however, attracted by the rich herbage of the meadows, has constituted the permanent population of these secluded places.

One of the most beautiful of the natural parks in the Rocky Mountain region is Estes Park, Colorado, located at the foot of Long's Peak which is one of the loftiest (14,272) and most interesting of the entire Range. The Park is situated about 75 miles northwest from the city of Denver, and is reached by a railroad ride of 50 miles and a stage drive over the remaining distance. At Lyons, the terminus of the railroad, the strenuous journey by stage begins. The mountain road, as such, is good and accidents are unknown, but the feminine passenger, if she be timid or nervous, experiences a degree of terror scarcely equaled by a 'holdup,' as the horses apparently unrestrained, gallop madly through gulches or down the sharp pitches, which are interspersed throughout the long ascent, while the precipitous roadsides seem to threaten instant destruction. After a height of eight thousand and sixty-two feet has been attained, a descent of five hundred feet brings one to the lowest level of Estes Park.

As one reaches the brow of the hill immediately overlooking the Park, he pauses, spellbound by the beauty of the scene. The mighty range, "Rockribbed and ancient as the sun" towers in a semicircle against the "turquoise sky of Colorado." Next are grouped the foothills, gray with granite, or dark with evergreens, and at their feet, like gay rugs, are spread the glades of the Park, bright with myriads of summer flowers, while through the midst of this coloring a mountain stream is woven like a silver thread, the shrubbery along its sides forming narrow lines of green.

Some enterprising spirits, alive to the beauty of the Park, are projecting an automobile line, and it is hoped that in the near future, the grade will be rendered much less by partially abandoning the present stage route, and the time of making the journey from Lyons to the Park will be reduced from five hours to two hours or less...

...The centre of the Park's enterprise and fashion is the somewhat straggling "Corners." At the first "Corner," a grocery store sets forth varied attractions, and at the blacksmith's shop and cobblers bench, man and beast may be shod "while you wait." At the second corner, is the post office, and the postmaster's residence, a store and telephone both for summer use only. There is also a humble building where during the warm weather, the venerable preacher of the mountains, of a Sunday exhorts his hearers, and where on weekdays, at scant portions of the year, knowledge is dispensed to the few children the stork ventures to bring to this isolated spot. During the "season," the "Corners" is a scene of life and gayety, when at nightfall, the stage comes in with the mail and passengers. The whole Park pours forth to meet it—ranchmen on their broncos, rigs from the scattered hotels, young men and maidens, usually on horseback—all chattering and laughing, for in "no time" everybody knows everybody else, and the pleasant expectancy of "getting the mail" puts each one in good humor.

The Park is too far removed from the big towns and cities to attract a large number of guests, and the half dozen small hotels with their environment of tents and cabins, comfortably provide for the summer visitors whose chief want is an outdoor life, uninterrupted by bad weather or the demands of society. To realize complete enjoyment of life in the mountains, one should know how to ride a bronco in order to take the trails that lead to peaks and glaciers; but the picnics, which are a favorite pastime, even the tenderfoot can join. Along the banks of streams are level stretches, shaded by magnificent pines, ideal spots for picnickers. Invariably, there are skillful anglers in the party. A mess of fish is caught, a fire is built from resinous pine boughs, and soon the air is fragrant with frying fish and bacon and steaming coffee. Upon the ground a snowy cloth is spread, and decorated with the flowers and greenery close at hand. The hampers are unpacked, the picnickers stroll in from walks and talks, and seating themselves Turkish fashion around the improvised board, "fall to." What deliciousness! What appetites! What wit and laughter! O, happy days long to be remembered.

Estes Park, whose longest axis is ten miles, is divided by the lay of the land into smaller parks. These natural enclosures form ranches where beeves are raised for market. Frequently those designed for slaughter are sent in autumn to the valley below to be quickly fattened on the richer herbage and the beet refuse left from the manufacture of sugar. To an Easterner, accustomed to see cattle comfortably stabled, the life of ranch stock seems one of hardship. With the coming of cold weather, the grasses are sear and dead. The chilling winds blow, the snows descend, and in all that desolation the cattle must find their own shelter, and much of their living, for the grass ranches are few and the hay produced is not proportionate to the stock. The dairy interests are very limited, and the calves follow their mothers all the season, instead of drawing their consolation from a scout bucket of skimmed milk after the manner of New England "bossies." The weeds which the household "mooley" crops often impart an unpalatable flavor to the milk, and sometimes I was mystified by the odor and taste of carbolic acid, and I was told it was due to a certain weed, which "mooley" seems to consider a great delicacy. The tubercular patient depends largely for his diet upon milk, cream and fresh eggs. The latter was very difficult to obtain until I organized a campaign. I instituted a house to house canvas. I chased everybody in the Park who owned a hen—but the hens seemed to be moulting or not doing very well. Then I offered a big advance in price, and "biddy" finally "shelled out," until I really had an embarrassment of eggs — I had corned the market.

The shortness of the season denied to their lofty lands the delicious round of cultivated fruits and berries and succulent plants, but underground vegetables flourish, especially potatoes which are so exceedingly toothsome, that one regrets man can not live by potatoes alone. If the soil does not cater sumptuously to the palate, it feasts the eye with the wide variety and beauty of wild flowers which luxuriate from the brookside to the arid rocks. The bloom of the loco weed, which crazes cattle if they crop it, colors acres of ground a rich magenta hue. The delicate... monkshood, columbine, the blue gentian, the sweet wild rose, every size and shade apparently of the helianthus and aster families, and countless other varieties lend their beauty to the glory of summer days. The frosts, which often come in the height of their bloom, only seem to make them brighter. When one remembers that the timber line of Mt. Washington, N.H. is less than four thousand feet above sea level, one can but marvel that vegetation should be so luxuriant in this spot, 7,500 feet above sea level, while the timber line is between three and four thousand feet higher. Groups of stately pines are disposed about the Park as if arranged by a landscape gardener, and forests of evergreen clamber up the hillsides. Here and there are little maple bushes, but the only deciduous <u>tree</u> I have noticed is the aspen which grows to a small size. Thickets of them fill up the draws of the hillsides giving touches of most brilliant green, and when the autumn frosts hasten the ripening of the quivering leaves, they glow amid the somberness of the pines like fields of buttercups.

During the month of July, there was a shower every day excepting two, and on one of those days it snowed. It was on the third of July when the peaks hid themselves in clouds, and blew out flurries of snow, while the mercury ran down to wintery figures. The thunderstorms were the most terrific of any I ever witnessed, although the old and permanent residents insist that the storms are not violent. There seemed to be a rivalry amongst the peaks in the thundershower business, and when one started up, the others formed in, till the blackness of night spread over us, and a roar and crash like a mighty battle deafened one. The vivid flashes of lightning simultaneous with the booming thunder, the rush and rattle of wind and rain conspired to strike terror to a timid soul. In a few moments this uproar ceased, the sun and the thirsty soil drank up the moisture, and in an hour or two, it was as arid as ever.

There were no dews, no mists except once when a heavy effacing fog preceded a snowstorm. This storm began on the fourteenth of September, and continued two days. How can I describe our sufferings! Ours was for summer housekeeping only, and its unplastered walls were covered with canvas or paper, its ceilings were of cotton cloth, paneled with strips of wood, and our heating apparatus consisted of a fireplace in the living room, and a stove in the isolated region of the kitchen. When this storm came roaring down the mountains, our house afforded us about as much protection as a tent. As the gusts swept through it, the ceilings rose and fell like the waves of ocean, and the flapping of canvas added a realism almost to the verge of seasickness. Fortunately I had brought flannels for my invalid, but Esther, my

Swedish maid, looked purple and goosefleshed in her summer attire as she trudged in and out bringing fagots for the fire. When I asked her if she were very cold, she plaintively answered, "My feets is cold." Luckily I was able to provide for the "feets." At night we piled everything upon our beds except the dishes, surrounded ourselves with hot water bottles and whatever other portable heating apparatus we could find, while Esther took the whole ironing outfit to bed with her. After the storm, the hills and mountains looked like great white billows, heaving up to the sky, and trees and shrubs were lost to view in the prevailing whiteness; but two or three days of September sun and wind took away every vestige of snow except from the Range.

When a day of Colorado's ideal weather came, we sat on the verandas, "united our souls" and wondered why the good Lord did not make every day as beautiful. As for employment, we did nothing, absolutely nothing, as the days were not long enough in which to do it. It was sufficient to revel in this delicious idleness, and watch the play of light and shade on the snow-patched mountains, — the rosy glow of morning, the white glare of noontide, the tender light of evening, with the violet and purple deepening in the shadows of the hills. The twilights linger in that altitude, and long after sundown, one would see masses of bright clouds, boiling up from the horizon.

The sounds that pass in the night at the Park are sometimes startling. One night, I was awakened by a strange, steady rumbling, like a railroad train. The house shook, the windows rattled, and my first thought was that one of the huge boulders airily poised in our backyard had toppled over, and was crashing into the cottage. But the next morning when we met at the Corners, everybody was asking, "Did you hear the earthquake?" And each threw into his recital such flourishes as his heated fancy suggested, till we wondered we had not been swallowed up in the convulsion, though it was true that rocks were dislodged. Another sound that often roused one from sleep was the howling of coyotes, weird and dreadful, as if Berbers, who guards the mouth of hell had not been given his customary Cerebus. Usually the nights were most serene, and in that clear atmosphere, the constellations seemed to hang down like great chandeliers, and the moon riding high in the heavens, gave a touch of awe and mystery to the wild landscape which it partially revealed.

Our solitude was gladden, by our dear little fourfooted friends the ground squirrels, who burrowed the soil and frolicked in the rocks about us. They were most neighborly when the seductive peanut and our personal fascinations had overcome their timidity. About twenty of them came at our call and sat upon our knees, or rummaged our pockets and the folds of our garments for peanuts. Anything more formidable from the wild was rarely seen. The elk is exterminated, the deer has gone across the range, and the castanets of the "rattler" are never heard. The wolf or the mountain lion sometimes prowls hungrily around the tender offspring of the herds, and the bear is not an impossible trophy of the gun or trap.

The solemn brooding of the mountains, and the sternness of the hills seem to influence the character of those who have lived continuously amid these impressive surroundings. The children seemed to me serious and thoughtful beyond their years and their communications were of scriptural brevity. I must except one child, (who brought me chickens and eggs), who conversed, but never chattered after the manner of children. One member of my family, possessing pedagogic instincts, could not refrain from questioning the child after the formula of the schoolmaster. "What town do you live in?" "Estes Park." "What county?" "Larimer." "What state?" "Colorado." "Who is the chief officer of the state?" "George Washington was till he died," replied the child, "and I don't know, who is now?" The store-keeper's daughter, a girl of 12 years, excited my wonder and admiration by her great capability. She tended store, and when her father was gone, took full charge, save that when her mother sauntered in with the baby. She weighed and measured, cast up accounts, tended the telephone, delivered messages, disciplined the younger children, and chewed gum as if nothing else was doing.

Estes Park is a bachelor's paradise. The isolation, and the dreariness of the cold season render it an undesirable residence for women the year round, and their number is less than the male population.

Some of these bachelors came from choice, and have taken up claims, others have been driven hither by the pitiless scourge of consumption. Some of them do their own house-keeping, or 'batch it' as they term it. Among them are men of education and culture, who have traveled the world over in search of health, and have found it only in the wilds of Colorado. In winter, they return to primitive. They grow beards, smoke heavy pipes, and tramp about in dreadful boots and rough clothes. But when the hope of the summer girl flutters in their breasts, the whiskers are reduced to natty mustachios, the more fetching clothes are donned, and various small refinements are practiced—all showing that the susceptibility to feminine charm is not lost.

At the time we left the Park, the days were full of autumnal splendor, and of nights the harvest moon lay ripening in the September skies, big and yellow and mellow. As we drove away, the mountains in their snowy cowls seemed to bow us a stately farewell, the somber pines waved us a mournful adieu; but the brook laughing and chattering, had no good byes to say, for it went with us down the steep hillsides on its way to gladden the plains below.

CHAPTER EIGHT
The Story of Grand Lake
By Mary Lyons Cairns and Enos A. Mills

The similarity between the community life and interests of the Estes Park and the Grand Lake regions, and the fact that they are destined to be brought into closer contact with the development of better connecting roads and increased travel, makes it seem desirable to include "The Story of Grand Lake" in the present volume.

Grand Lake is the largest natural lake in Colorado. It is situated in Middle Park and the village of Grand Lake is clustered about its shores. The lake is elliptical in outline; a trifle more than a mile wide by two miles long; and its depth over the deeper portion is given at from 250 to 700 feet. This lake lies in the western boundary of the Rocky Mountain National Park, at an elevation of about 8,500 feet, and almost directly west of Long's Peak. Many thrilling frontier incidents have been staged at Grand Lake. One incident worthy of remembering is that the expedition which first made the summit of Long's Peak, outfitted at this place.

The first white men probably came to Grand Lake in the latter eighteen fifties. Two or three small cabins were built about that time by hunters and fishermen. The first permanent white settler, however, was Joseph L. Wescott (familiarly known as "Judge") who came in 1867, built a cabin on the west shore of the lake not far from the present site of the Henry Hanington cottage, and was for many years "master of all he surveyed." He had fought as a Union cavalryman through the Civil war, and came to Colorado immediately after he was mustered out of the service, settling first at Hot Sulphur Springs in 1865.

Wescott was a well informed man, and his listeners were entertained for hours at a time with his talks on astronomy, as well as his tales of adventure and hardship. He hunted, fished and trapped for a living, and an occasional trip to the outside world across the range, to sell furs and buy provisions, filled years of his life. At times he prospected, and always firmly believed that some day he would surely "strike it." Many times he suffered extreme privation.

As years passed and the trappers and prospectors became more numerous, the need of a post office was felt and Judge Wescott was Grand Lake's first Postmaster. It is told that the post office equipment consisted only of a canned goods box; the mail was put into it, and whoever came for his mail sorted over the pile, took what was his, and conscientiously replaced the rest for the next comer.

No Native Americans lived at the Lake after Judge Wescott came, though he often met friendly Utes, when hunting or trapping in different parts of Middle Park. A few scattered arrow heads have been picked up, and a whetstone was once found by James Cairns near the site of his old store. From some of the Utes Judge Wescott learned the legend of the Lake, a story which interests visitors to this day.

THE LEGEND OF THE LAKE

One summer, many years ago, before the pale-faces came, a large number of Ute Indians were camped on the shores of Grand Lake, when the Arapahoe and the Cheyenne (affiliated tribes) made a sudden and fierce attack upon them. On the southwest side of the lake, overlooking a vast area of Middle Park, is a very high rock called "Lookout Point," from which an approaching party may be seen for miles. As this was the usual station of the Native scouts, it is difficult to understand why the Utes did not know of the approach of the Cheyenne and the Arapahoe. At any rate, in the ensuing battle very few escaped. About three hundred Ute braves were killed. Tradition has it, that just before the battle all the Ute squaws and papooses were placed upon a raft and sent out on the lake for safety. A treacherous wind came down from the gulches, the raft was overturned, and all were drowned. The loss of so many warriors of the tribe and the death of the women and the children caused a superstition regarding the region to be transmitted from one generation to another. In is a significant fact that from that day to this the Ute Indians have avoided Grand Lake with an aversion born of intense fear, mingled with feelings of deepest sorrow.

The famous rock in the bathing beach of the lake, "Minnie's Altar," was named for Miss Minnie Proctor. Miss Proctor was the character represented by "Kady" in Patience Stapleton's book of that name. Her brother, Phinester P. Proctor, called "Pheme" by the early residents, spent his childhood in Grand Lake. He is now a famous sculptor and lives in New York City. On one of Mrs. Stapleton's visits to Grand Lake she talked with Wescott and from him gathered many of the incidents upon which her story was based. Judge Wescott plays a prominent part in the character of "Judge West."

Judge Wescott never married, but lived alone until practically the time of his death, which occurred in the fall of 1914.

Through the seventies and early eighties single men and men with families began to populate the west and north shores of Grand Lake, and a mining boom in the country to the northwest caused two towns to spring up with great rapidity. The town of Lulu, about twenty miles away, had over forty voters; Gaskill, seven miles distant, had seventy-five; while Grand Lake had about one hundred and fifty. The town of Grand Lake was surveyed in 1881, and James Cairns erected the first building—a store—on the new townsite.

The new mining boom quickly populated the village, cabins sprang up here and there, and all was excitement and industry. The Grand Lake Mining and Smelting Company was formed, this company owning mines in both Baker and Bowen Gulches. Among them were the "Wolverine," "Toponas," "Sandy Campbell," "Lone Star," "Manxman," and "Jim Bowen."

In April, 1881, the county seat was moved from Hot Sulphur Springs to Grand Lake, and remained there until November, 1888. The County Court House and the Jail, crude as they were, still stand, but long since have been used for other purposes.

From 1882 to 1889 the town boasted a newspaper called "The Grand Lake Prospector." A few copies are still treasured by pioneers, and are very interesting reading for the younger generation. "The Prospector" was edited by John Smart and the late George W. Bailey. During Bailey's residence at Grand Lake he studied law and was admitted to the bar. He afterwards was elected Judge of the Supreme Court of Colorado, as was also the late Judge Charles F. Caswell, who was County Attorney for a time while the County Seat was at Grand Lake.

It was while the County Seat was at Grand Lake that the following tragic political feud occurred: About eight o'clock in the morning of July Fourth, 1883, a few villagers, perhaps ten or twelve, in James Cairns' store plainly heard a number of shots, but paid very little attention thinking that someone was harmlessly celebrating the Fourth. About twenty minutes later a stranger, who had arrived in town the day before, came into the store, excitedly telling them that several men had been shot on the west shore of the Lake. Hurriedly harnessing a team to a wagon, several men drove at once to the scene of the tragedy. John J. Mills and Barney Day, both members of the Board of County Commissioners, were found dead, Mills having been shot through the brain and Day in the heart. Mr. Weber, the third Commissioner, was badly wounded in the lungs and died about twelve o'clock the same night. Captain Dean, acting County Clerk, was wounded in one hip and lived only ten days.

The old Fairview Hotel still stands on "Craig's Point" and is a place of interest for its many early associations. The first hotel in Grand Lake was the "Grand Lake House," built before the townsite was surveyed. It was erected in 1878 or 1879 by Wilson Waldron who came to Grand Lake with his wife and three children about this date. Today it stands crooked with the street, crazy, ramshackle, unoccupied, with only the ghosts of by-gone days to whisper tales of merry-making and joy, trouble and misery.

The big dining-room of the Grand Lake House was the scene of many a jolly dance. The old-time dances were truly western affairs, scenes of hearty hospitality such as are seldom found except in pioneer communities. During the "boom" days at Grand Lake when the mines were in operation, there were often as many as three, four and five dances a week during the winter. People came from all over Middle Park on horseback, in sleighs, and even on snowshoes, and it was not an uncommon sight to see the men in overalls, blue flannel shirts and high mining boots.

Old John Mitchell, a trapper, was for many years the sole musician at the Grand Lake dances, and the fervor with which he entered into his playing added much to the zest of these occasions. "I can see him yet," said someone not long ago, "sitting high above the dancers on a platform, his fiddle under his chin, his foot keeping time to the music, a smile on his face and a look in his eyes that told plainly his rapture had carried him far away from the sordidness of life. Quadrilles and the Virginia Reel— those were our dances—and when the fiddle played its loudest and best for the dancers, down the long room the dancers would come, laughing and singing. Yes, those were the good old days."

Reminiscences of pioneer days always include tales of ferocious bears, and one of these stories—that of Charlie Hedrick's encounter—is still vivid in the minds of the early settlers. Charlie Hedrick, a boy about sixteen years of age, lived with his father and mother on a ranch located on the North Fork of the Grand River, almost opposite Bowen Gulch. A man who had recently come out from Indiana decided to go trapping with Charlie, and the two built a trap—an old-time log trap or house—in Baker Gulch about three miles from home.

One morning, alert and expectant, the boy and the man started for the trap, and were delighted to find in it a two-year-old Silver Tip bear. From the tracks around the trap, and from the torn and scratched condition of the young trees, they could see that the father and mother bears had been there. Leaving the young bear in the trap, the man and the boy went up a hill to look for the parent bears. The bears espied them, and with furious force the mother bear attacked the Hedrick boy. The male stood off about a hundred feet, and eventually ran away. Rushing upon Charlie, the mother bear struck him with her claws, broke his jaw, split his lower lip and tore out some of his teeth. She clutched his throat in her teeth and bit him badly in the neck. Realizing that he was overpowered, Charlie called for the man who shot the bear twice with his horse-pistol before the bear let go her hold of the boy. Then snatching Charlie's rifle, the man shot the bear and killed her. He carried the boy back home and immediately sent to Grand Lake for help. This was in April and the snow was too deep for them to get a buggy to the house. Charlie was carried three-quarters of a mile on the crusted snow and then placed in a buggy and taken to Grand Lake. The following morning he was taken to a Denver Hospital, where he finally recovered from his wounds.

The first school was held in the east end of the Nickerson cottage, during the winter of 1881-82. Miss McGee, a niece of Wilson Waldron, was the teacher. There were about twenty-four pupils at that time, made up of children of the Proctor, Nickerson, Waldron, and David Cairns families.

The first marriage was that of Henry Schiveley (known as Hank) and Miss McGee. This occurred early in the summer of 1882, after the close of the school term.

The first white child born at Grand Lake was Roy Waldron, son of Mr. and Mrs. Wilson Waldron, in April, 1880. The second child born was Willard Johnston, son of Mr. and Mrs. Thomas H. Johnston, November 8, 1881. This happened to be election day and was also made memorable by a heavy fall of snow. The weather continued stormy and cold, and the snow that fell that day did not melt away until late the next spring.

The first white death at Grand Lake was the accidental drowning of a man by the name of Cole, during the summer of 1871. The first natural death was that of Mrs. Simmonds, mother of Mrs. Schaffer. She was a very old lady, and died from the general effects of old age, in 1880. Down below the Sagebrush Flat is a little neglected cemetery, where the early-day burials were made. In this little burying ground the bodies of Mrs. Simmonds, Mr. Winslow Nickerson and his wife, Lillian, Commissioner J. G. Mills, and two prospectors, "Doc" Dudy and Bob Plummer lay.

During the winter of 1883-84 winter sports were introduced into the village by the County Clerk, a Scandinavian by the name of Jehrn. Sleds were in general use, but skiing was the popular sport, and men, women and children enjoyed the fun to the utmost. The favorite run, especially when the crowd went out at night, was from the top of the steep moraine, back of the Arghalier cottage, down to the main street. These sports have been revived by the present generation, but they have been entered into with no greater zeal than in the days of the early settlers.

The early history of Grand Lake if filled with stories of privation, hardship, danger, had a sprinkling of comedy. All honor is due the sturdy pioneers, men and women alike, who fought the fight, often desperately lonely, many times hungry, struggling through the long, snowy winters for the upbuilding of their homes and the community. It is not all a story of hardship and calamity, however. The pioneers say now that "the good old times" are past, and that none of the present generation can even imagine the joy and pleasure of the dances they had in the old days. People came for miles and miles, they danced all night, they sang together, and they coasted down the hills many and many a winter night with all the abandon of joyous youth.

The old days and the old ways are passing. Grand Lake is becoming a popular resort; new hotels are being built, and new costly summer cottages are springing up each year on the shores of this wonderful gem of Nature. Famous men and women come and go.

But the romantic beauty of it all cannot pass. The chugging of the motors and the buzz of automobiles may disturb the quietude; but for those who have eyes to see and ears to hear, the fairies will still dance in the moonlight in the Fairy Dell; the spirits of the Native warriors will still call above the roar of the rushing falls; and in the twilight one may even catch the sound of a lover calling to his maiden, and listening closely to the echoes that come back from Shadow Mountain, hear ever so softly, her answer.

LEGEND OF GRAND LAKE
By Judge Joseph L. Wescott

"White man, pause and gaze around,
　　for we tread the haunted ground."
So said a chief to me one day,
　　as along the shore we wound our way.
"On the same ground where we now stand,
　　once was encamped a happy band;
One hundred warriors as true and brave
　　as ever slept in warrior's grave;
Cheikiwow, chief, had given command
　　that every warrior of the band
Should arm and be prepared to fight,
　　for danger hovered about that night.
The whole wide heavens were overcast,
　　and nearer came the howling blast;
The bright forked lightning wildly flashed,
　　and deep-toned thunders loudly crashed;
Now from afar came the grey wolf's howl
　　and the dismal hoot of the big horned owl.
But hark! another cry we hear,
　　that fills our hearts with boding fear—
That well-known cry so sharp and shrill
　　is the clear-cut note of the whippoorwill;
Scarce had its echoes died away
　　when there appeared in fierce array,
And from every rock and shrub arose
　　the fierce Cheyennes and Arapahoes.
Then from each painted warrior's throat
　　arose a defiant wild war note,
And at the moment a drenching rain
　　burst over lake and rock and plain.
The arrowy tempest fell around
　　and struck the trees and rocks and ground;
But others, more true, with deadly aim,
　　stretched warriors bleeding on the plain,
Both friends and foes were falling fast,
　　as thick as snow in winter blast.
The foeman's chief, Red Wolf by name,
　　a leader with a giant frame,
It was his boast that no single foe

could cope with him with spear or bow.
That bloodstained chief that fearful night
  met Cheikiwow in single fight.
Each chieftain stood transfixed, amazed;
  each at the other sternly gazed.
Then high aloft each held his hand,
  and the battle ceased at their command.
Each warrior's spear was levelled low,
  lowered at once was each drawn bow.
The barbed shaft sped through the sky,
  but from their shields dropped harmless by.
Again and still again they shot,
  but shields each time their missiles caught;
The useless bow was cast aside,
  the fatal spear its place supplied.
The cold sweat stood on Red Wolf's brow;
  he met his match in Cheikiwow.
At last from Cheikiwow a dextrous stroke,
  and Red Wolf's spear was shattered and broke.
But Cheikiwow, you all must know,
  would never strike an unarmed foe;
He threw his spear against a rock,
  and it was broken by the shock;
Then each chieftain drew his knife,
  continuing the deadly strife.
The last fierce thrust that Red Wolf made
  was by Cheikiwow quickly stayed—
His knife flashed like a flaming dart,
  and pierced the Red Wolf to the heart.
Black Bear, the second in command,
  is now the leader of the band.
We strove in vain our chief to save,
  to spare him from a bloody grave.
'Exterminate this hostile tribe;
  leave not a single foe alive!'
He cried in accents fierce and loud,
  to his wild and murderous crowd:
'Cast every spear, spring every bow,
  against Cheikiwow and lay him low';
Against that single manly form
  showered that fearful, deadly storm.
His gallant form was failing fast,
  those sinewy limbs must yield at last,
And weakened by many a ghastly wound,

fainting he fell upon the ground.
But ere the spark of life had fled
    he rose as if up from the dead,
And once more raised his axe on high,
    then rang his last fierce battle cry.
When we beheld our leader fall,
    a frenzied shout rose from us all.
We bore our chieftain's form away—
    it were suicide to longer stay.
A weak spot in our foeman's ranks,
    where death had played its direst pranks,
From where I stood I now espied,
    and calling my comrades to my side,
I bade them quickly follow me
    in one grand dash for liberty.
Up yonder rugged mountain side,
    with rapid pace I quickly hied.
And upon a beetling rock I stood
    and gazed upon the angry flood.
Between dark clouds the moon shone out,
    throwing its silver light about;
The wind still blew with solemn roar,
    the angry waves still lashed the shore.
When night her mantle has shed around
    the silent forms of earth and ground,
The ghosts of those dead warriors slain,
    rise from out their graves again;
Again in battle line they stand,
    the dead chief leading his command;
But at the first faint streak of day
    these ghostly forms quick fade away.
Behold this lock, now seen so white,
    in one short hour was changed that night."

The chieftain ceased—his tale was told
    of scenes that happened in days of old,
And night had settled on lake and plain
    when we returned to our camp again.

PLEASE HELP

In every region visited by picnickers and campers the problem is to prevent the mutilation or the destruction of the attractions, and to keep the region free of refuse. Visitors as well as local people can help maintain the charm and cleanness of our outing wilderness by packing out all camp refuse,—tin cans, lunch boxes, bags, and chocolate papers.

The cutting of the picturesque and ancient trees at timberline, the uprooting, and the excessive gathering of wild flowers have already seriously scarred many near-by places of enjoyment.

Whenever requested, children cheerfully respond and do their best to leave camp sites clean and unscarred. Realizing that elder folks will also help, this appeal is made to them. It is easy to understand that an enemy of our country should want to destroy its attractiveness. Everyone may show his love of native land without desiring to kill a foreign foe. We believe that every good American will respond to the general appeal now being made throughout the land to protect and perpetuate our parks and wild garden outing places.

ROCKY MOUNTAIN NATIONAL PARK

The Rocky Mountain National Park is a marvelous grouping of gentleness and grandeur; a wilderness mountain world of groves and grass plots, crags and canyons, rounded lakes with shadow-matted shores that rest in peace within the purple forest. There are wild flowers of every color and many a silken meadow edged with ferns. Brokenness and beauty, terrace upon terrace, a magnificent hanging wild garden; an eloquent wordless hymn, sung in silent, poetic pictures. Over these terraces waters rush and pour. From ice-sculptured, snow-piled peaks, young and eager streams leap in white cascades between crowding cliffs and pines. Through this wilderness winds the trail, with its secrets of the centuries, where adventures come and go and where the magic camp-fire blossoms in the night. In these primeval scenes the grizzly bear gives to the wilderness its master spell; the mountain ram poses on the cliff; the laughing, varied voice of the coyote echoes when the afterglow falls; the home-loving beaver builds his willow-fringed hut; the birds sing; the cheerful chipmunk frolics and never grows up; and here the world stays young.

Trail Card Series Number Four

AN APPRECIATION
by Judge Ben Lindsey

Like all great men, Enos Mills was perhaps least appreciated while he lived—and however much that appreciation was—I think all will agree that Mills, his work and what he stood for, cannot be too much known and understood. It means far more to our children than the work of men after whom many of our mountain peaks have been named. Some of these men like Zebulon Pike, discovered the bodies of our mountains. Mills discovered their souls. In the sordid struggle of commercialism largely to enrich themselves, men have discovered their mineral wealth. Mills discovered there a far greater wealth—one that may be shared with all mankind. He found there the sweet stories of the trees, the romance of the woods, and all living creatures that inhabit those temples of God. He had brought them to light through marvelous understanding, he did this in his lectures and happily in the books he has left for us and our children. Here we may find the real poetry, music and philosophy of life. Or, rather, here we may find the touchstone, the inspiration, the way to Heaven on Earth. His insight and understanding of life as it is, as interpreted through God's living things, will make for us a better citizenship.

Let us resolve that the soul of those mountains shall not be commercialized by the touch of men's greed that broke his heart...the heart that is the heart of the hills, the soul of nature, the touch of God.

October 5, 1922

Mrs. Enos Mills,
Longs Peak, Colorado

My dear Mrs. Mills,-

Judge Lindsey and I appreciate
very much your letter of September 30. Indeed Judge
Lindsey considered it a privilege to pay the last
tribute to such a splendid man as Mr. Mills.

The Judge wishes me to tell you
that he did not prepare his little talk and so he
has none of it written down. He spoke that day
just from the depth of his own heart. I think the
Rocky Mountain News had some excerpts from it, but
doubtless you have already secured their article.

With sincere regards,

Very truly yours,

Henrietta B. Lindsey.

The Story of Estes Park

AND

A Guide Book

BY ENOS A. MILLS

CONTAINS the history of Estes Park from the days of Kit Carson, in 1840, to 1905, together with pioneer incidents and experiences.

The Guide Book has excellent descriptions of Estes Park, Long's Peak, the glaciers, the old volcano, and the woods, lakes, flowers and other natural beauties and attractions.

It recounts some of the amusing and serious experiences of climbers on Long's Peak and tourists in the Park. It has many valuable hints and suggestions.

There are three dozen beautiful half-tone pictures.

The book contains a list of hotels and their prices, together with milage and altitude tables.

In it is folded a large map, which shows the location of peaks, streams, hotels and the trails.

The book has an appropriate cover design, is artistic and thoroughly first class in every respect. It is well worthy of beautiful Estes Park.

Size 5x8 3-8, Cloth $1.50.   Paper $1.25.

Published by **OUTDOOR LIFE,** Denver, Colo.

At Long's Peak Inn

YOU WILL HEAR THE

Call of the Wild.

Nature will be your neighbor.

Higher than any hotel in the Alps.

Above troubleline and near timberline and snow.

The place to meet LONG'S PEAK and see the Rockies.

TRAILS to the silent places and the heights.

Evergreens and their rich aroma.

No consumptives taken.

The house stands by a mountain brook in a wild flower garden.

Fringed blue gentians and columbines.

Comfort and home flavored meals.

Pine knots blaze in the big fire place.

ENOS A. MILLS,

ESTES PARK,   COLORADO.

SPRAGUE'S

It is the desire and aim of the proprietor of Sprague's to conduct a place as far from hotel life and as home-like as possible. We not only have a large, new rustic hotel, but many cosy cottages.

Wild Flowers and Pines at the door. Good Fishing within five minutes' walk.

There are peaks and canons near at hand for exploration. But if you want to wander far away, we can outfit you with an outfit and guides. Eight miles will take you across "the range'" to the Pacific slope.

NEARER

Specimen Mountain, Sprague's Glacier, Glacier Gorge, Flattop Trail and Grand Lake than any other hotel, and just as near to Long's Peak and Hallet Glacier.

The Bungalow is a delightful place for hops or entertainments, and is also an ideal place to have a chat by the fireplace.

We do not take consumptives.

Our livery is one of the best in Estes or Moraine Parks.

References can be given in nearly every city in the United States.

J. D. STEAD, Propr.,

MORAINE PARK,   *COLORADO.*

ELKHORN
LODGE
ESTES PARK

*A first-class summer resort within
seven miles of perpetual snow.
All modern improvements.*

Centrally located.

Good trout fishing, also hunting in season.

All kinds of game within one half day's ride.

Golfing, Tennis and other amusements.

Good Livery in connection.

Also nicely furnished cottages for house-keeping.

*Prices and descriptive matter
on application.*

Mrs. W. E. James & Sons,
Proprietors.

Made in the USA
San Bernardino, CA
30 May 2018